High Performance Human Capital Leadership

THE ALLEN AUSTIN WAY

*Real World Solutions for Hiring
and Retaining CEOs & Executive Talent
in 2011 and Beyond*

ROB ANDREWS
&
THE PARTNERS OF
ALLEN AUSTIN
GLOBAL EXECUTIVE SEARCH

High Performance Human Capital Leadership
Copyright © 2011

Author: Robert L. Andrews
Printed and bound by Lulu Publishing
Cover photo - ©iStockphoto.com/Mickey_man

Paperback ISBN: 978-0-557-58128-3
Hardcover ISBN: 978-0-257-05271-4

I would like to dedicate this work to all of the incredible and

devoted search professionals who comprise Allen Austin.

They are the smartest, most talented group of individuals

with whom I have ever had the pleasure to work.

I would also like to mention my original mentor

in the search profession without whom

I never would have had the opportunity

to experience the profession which has become my passion,

Larry Gladstone.

And as an appeal to boards, CEOs and General Managers

that there is nothing more important in business

than taking personal responsibility for the attraction,

selection, hiring, retaining, coaching, mentoring

and developing human capital.

Forward

I wrote this book at the encouragement and in some cases insistence of a number of CEOs, board members, and human resource professionals who told me that this material was desperately needed. The book is and will be a work in progress as long as I am active. I add, delete and revise material almost daily in order to provide maximum value.

If you have purchased a copy of this book, I will be happy to send you a copy with the updates at any time.

In my view, the executive hiring process typically works like dating and marriage, with very similar results. Just like dating, we usually start out with a woefully inadequate description of precisely who we are, exactly what we are looking for, and specifically what we are trying to accomplish.

Because we usually rely on simple job descriptions and resumes, we typically do not define all of the critical success factors in advance, as well as our specific performance objectives; and because we do not fast forward the tape and look in to the future, the selection process becomes a beauty pageant and a chemistry contest. We hire a new executive because it feels right; he or she looks good, sounds good, smells good, and is, oh so charming. Then, in three to six months, we start to have that queasy feeling in our gut that suggests we might have made a mistake and that things are just not working out. Roughly 50 percent of the time, within a year, we know we have made a mistake.

For more than thirty years, I have studied what is currently being called human capital leadership. Buzz words, trends, and pop expressions come and go. What I am really talking about in this piece is getting things done with and through people: attracting, screening, selecting, hiring, leading, managing, encouraging, disciplining, organizing, and retaining people.

It has been said that it takes 10,000 hours of study to become an expert in any subject. If that is true, I suppose thirty-five years of study makes me an expert although I do not particularly like the term. Especially since I have also heard that an *Ex* is a has-been and a *Spurt* is a drip under pressure.

The expert debate notwithstanding, I think you will get a great deal of real value out of this material. I have read hundreds of books on these subjects. I subscribe to all of the latest and greatest thought resources including the Harvard Business Review. I have also had the privilege of knowing and working with some unbelievably effective leaders and managers.

While I am an admitted contrarian on a number of issues, I believe the advice outlined in this material is extremely sound. I also know that the "business as usual" model does not work. My intent is to separate the wheat from the chaff, using as few words as possible, and without all of excerpts from articles and studies that have been saying the same thing for years, in order to present you with material that will help you with your real world human capital leadership endeavors.

I would also like to make it very clear that I am critical of how the hiring process works in general terms. It is not my intention to say disparaging things about any firm in particular or my profession in general. My hope is that you will read these words and examine your own human capital practices.

Where My Journey Started

I became interested in business and leadership at a very young age for reasons that remain unclear. Somewhere in my hardwiring, resided an intense curiosity about the way organizations are staffed and led. My first job was in a convenience store where I outlasted five different store managers and had an opportunity to observe how not to manage a business enterprise. My second job was in a small independent grocery store where I survived three management changes and yet more examples of what did and did not work.

In July of 1970 I turned sixteen and was old enough to work legally. Having four years of full-time food retailing experience, I went to work for Safeway Stores, Inc. in one of Houston's earliest Safeway stores. By July of 1972, I had performed just about every job available in a food store and was promoted to Management Trainee. In 1974, I became an Assistant Store Manager and was promoted to Store Manager in 1975.

During the nine years I spent with Safeway, I received an absolutely spectacular education on what leadership is and is not. I also learned much about management; what good management looked like and non-existent management looked like. I saw outstanding leadership combined with pretty good management produce great results. I saw tight management with mediocre leadership produce lousy results. Then I had the distinct pleasure of seeing the spectacular results stemming from good management and outstanding leadership.

In 1978, I got my first real exposure to what happens in a substantial organization when you replace a great leader with a micromanager with lousy leadership skills. February of 1978 I saw my hero, a great leader named Don Gates, who had led our division as Retail Operations Manager since its inception, promoted to Division Manager in Butte, Montana.

Don Gates was a fiery and passionate retailing executive who epitomized high performance leadership. He was a high school graduate who often talked about spending ten years as a produce department manger. Don was hardly the typical executive you would see described in a modern day search spec and yet he had every attribute necessary in order to be an exemplary leader.

When Don left our division to take over the reins in Butte, a thirty-nine store division regarded by many as a starter division, he made dramatic improvements in store performance and the division made money for the first time in many years. He left the Butte division to take over the Kansas City division where he repeated his stellar performance.

Don's next stop was the Southern California division, the largest division in the company, where he set records for same-store sales and profits as well as overall Return on Investment performance. He was then asked to lead the Eastern Division, headquartered in Landover, Maryland and ultimately retired as Division President in Phoenix.

I make it a point to stop and talk about Don Gates for a number of reasons. First of all, leadership is not limited to, or just about degrees, years of experience, job titles, intelligence, pedigree, or technical expertise.

High performance leaders consistently lead in a manner that inspires others to trust and follow them. They know how to connect with the workforce in such a manner that everyone in the organization understands the mission at hand. They are involved in all of the critical areas of the business: strategy, people systems and operations. They are not micromanagers by any means, but they are fully aware of what is going on in their business. They understand what drives the business.

High performance leaders encourage their leadership teams to stretch and achieve while holding everyone accountable for his or her performance, behavior, and promises. High performance leaders, unlike managers, help their organizations cope with ambiguity by crystallizing the end objective, painting the vision, assigning priorities, separating the wheat from the chaff, and providing a laser-like focus. High performance leaders do not know it all; they know what they do not know. They understand their own strengths, weaknesses, and propensities; they delegate and compensate accordingly. High performance leaders share information, resources, and credit effectively. They understand there is no limit to what can be accomplished if they do not care who gets the credit.

High performance leaders are real people. They are not afraid to show vulnerability, admit mistakes, and ask for help. They are constantly communicating their company's vision, purpose, and values. High performance leaders are constantly mindful of customers, end users, and their rank-and-file employees. High performance leaders are decisive, not reckless. They understand that a good plan, well executed, beats an iron-clad plan with mediocre execution every time. These people understand that all employees deep down want to do a good job and want to feel like they are making a contribution. They understand that we are all looking for leadership.

High performance leaders are confident, yet not arrogant. They are in constant contact with their organization to the extent they can feel the pulse; their constituents feel a connection with them. High performance leaders have a sense of humor and the ability to make the job fun. They understand the power of a workforce that is happy to see them, not afraid of them. These individuals are high integrity players. They mean and do what they say; they have no hidden agendas. Most high performance leaders are story tellers. They teach by telling stories, using anecdotes and metaphors to illustrate their points and put things in perspective. These people instill passion in others and energize their workforces. They treat everyone with dignity and respect and do not tolerate abuse of others.

Don Gates exemplified all of these traits and I will always be grateful for his example. He was enormously impactful for many aspiring young leaders, such as myself. I will always be grateful for the exposure to such a powerful High Performance Leader early in my career. He helped me set a leadership standard that has been very helpful in assessing the effectiveness of my own leadership, as well as that of others.

CONTENTS

ONE

Search Firm Strategy

Facilitating a match that will truly work for the company and the candidate alike should be the primary goal of every executive search. We exist for the purpose of adding significant value to our client companies through our human capital consulting efforts *and* to enhance the lives and careers of our candidates (as well as our consultants). Our passion is facilitating matches that work and last.

Having spent twenty-four years in industrial management and nineteen years in executive search, I have made a lot of great hires and a few bad ones. I have seen every conceivable hiring mistake. I have seen the same hiring manager make the same hiring mistakes over and over again. I have seen entire companies make the same mistakes over and over and over again.

I have read literally hundreds of books on hiring, search, selection, interviewing, reference checking, background checking, and the like. Most of the material I have read is of very little use, either because it was entirely anecdotal and without basis in fact, or because it was purely theoretical in nature with little basis in reality.

Here is an actual example of a garden variety search to which I was a witness. The names have been changed to protect the guilty. Some literary license has been taken; yet the representation of relevant facts is substantially accurate.

John Q. CEO decides he is unhappy with Jack C. VP Operations' performance. Jack has been on the job for just under eighteen months and is a very hard worker. John is not able to clearly articulate just what it is about Jack he does not like; he simply says that things are not going well. He calls Dave C. Headhunter to schedule a meeting. Dave comes to mind first because he works for one of the top search firms downtown; he has also bought John's lunch twice, he has taken John to play golf at the top course in town and he sent John tickets for a sold-out play.

John and Dave get together for a luncheon meeting at the country club. They talk for an hour or so but not much is said about the search. Just prior to the conclusion of the meeting, John hands Dave a job description for the VP Operations position. Dave thinks the job description sounds familiar. It should. It is the same description given to Dave twenty months prior when he began the search which produced Jack C. Dave does not bother to seek specifics in terms of performance problems.

He shakes John's hand enthusiastically and with all the confidence that generally comes with ignorance he says "Do not worry John, I know you and your organization, I will find you the right guy." Dave is still looking John in the eye while thinking "Does he remember I placed the guy he is about to fire?" and "I know two guys who would be perfect."

Dave gets back to his office and throws the job description on Greg C. Senior Associate's desk and instructs him to put together a search specification. Greg asks if anything has changed at John's company. Dave replies that everything is pretty much the same and instructs Greg to do some "cutting and pasting" to produce the "new spec." He also asks Greg to have a data base query run even though he thinks he already knows who the finalists will be. Greg runs the query and produces two more candidates who appear to fit the "new spec."

During the course of the next three months, Greg spends some time on the search but he is also working on seven others concurrently. Dave decides to go forward with the four semifinalists and schedules video conference interviews with each. All four interviews go well, but Dave elects to eliminate candidate number 4. He just does not have the personal presence of the other three, nor does he have a prestigious MBA as do the others. Dave prepares interview notes and presents his three finalists to John. John is very happy with the credentials he sees and asks Debbie, his administrative assistant, to schedule face to face interviews at corporate. Debbie will have to coordinate interview times with George K. CFO, Mark F. CIO, Mike D. CMO and Sam D. EVP HR.

The interviews begin the following week. All three candidates are invited to Corporate to interview with John, George, Mark, Mike, and Sam. There is a schedule for each senior officer, but no structure has been established nor discovery objectives assigned. George's interviews go fine although he could only spend about twenty minutes with Candidate 2 because he had a bank meeting that ran late. He favors Candidate 3 because he makes a strong personal presentation, has a Wharton MBA, and likes the Tampa Bay Buccaneers. Mark is only able to see candidates 1 and 3 because of an emergency meeting called with one of the firm's software vendors. He likes both candidates. He sees them as "pretty equal." Mike keeps all three of his appointments and tries to give each candidate careful consideration. He has concerns about candidate number 2; he seemed nervous and uncomfortable in the interview. His eye contact was not as consistent as the other two. Sam keeps all three of his appointments and uses a structured interview questionnaire. Sam determines that candidate number 2 is the most solid performer and is truly a good fit, but does not think he will pass muster with the others because his interviewing skills are weaker than his competitors.

When the powers meet, the decision is made to extend an offer to candidate number 3. The prevailing reasons – John thinks he is the most impressive; George likes his presence, his Wharton MBA, and his affection for the Buccaneers. Mark would go with number 1 or 3. Mike does not voice much support for number 1 or 3, just his concerns about number 2. Sam makes a case for candidate number 2, given his track record but is quickly shot down by the others.

The offer is extended and accepted by candidate number 3, Tom Jones, who starts work four weeks later and everyone is happy, as is Dave the recruiter, who has just sent his final invoice, bringing his total revenues for this search to just over $130,000. Everyone has high expectations of Tom.

Why? Why would the management team and the search consultant have any expectations of Tom? All they really know is that he seems to be a nice guy, has a Wharton MBA and is really impressive in person. What are the chances of Tom's success? Somewhere between 50 percent and 55 percent: marginally better than a flip of the coin.

I have witnessed these kinds of activities and the often disastrous results they produce more times than I care to imagine. Who do I blame? I guess I could blame our educational system. That seems to be popular these days. Well, the answer is either no one or everyone.

The fact of the matter is most executives do not know how to conduct an effective search. A surprising number of search professionals have not had any formal training in terms of how to conduct an effective search. Most of us are very good at everything we do except the search, selection, and hiring process. Once again, this should be no big surprise. Consider my background – twenty-four years in business with responsibility for two divisions with revenues in excess of $700 million each, combined with ten years in undergraduate and graduate schools. How many courses have been required to complete, or even offered, in academic institutions on hiring, selection, interviewing, et cetera? Zero. How much instruction was given during my twenty-four years in industry? I took one course on interrogation to determine whether or not the subject was being truthful.

A study published in a 2006 edition of the Harvard Business Review indicated that two of every five recently placed chief executives failed within eighteen months.

Other surveys we have read in recent years suggest that somewhere between 46 percent and 50 percent of all newly placed senior executives are fired or resign within two years. Such statistics and dismal results have prompted us to study the myriad of things that often go wrong during the executive search process. I should also add that quite a number of internal placements and promotions turn out badly as well.

Almost every business day since August 2, 1996, the day I founded Allen Austin, I have tried to isolate one failed executive placement and determine the reason for that particular failure. At the time of this writing, I have examined 3,033 CEO and executive level placements that failed. Here are some of the verbatim comments noted:

The placement went awry because:

THE HIRING AUTHORITY

- did not establish specific performance objectives for the new executive in his specific role

- did not understand and/or did not articulate the true drivers in the business

- did not understand and/or was not able to clearly articulate the values of her organization

- did not focus on the candidate's consistent and predictable patterns of relative success or lack thereof.

- did not understand the difference between management and leadership

- did not clearly articulate organizational nuances such as resource allocation, departmental influence or dominance, silo management and the like.

- did not clearly articulate what kinds of behaviors are valued and respected within the organization

- did not establish that the new candidate's career goals and objectives were aligned with those of the organization and that the new relationship represented a win-win for candidate and company

- did not ensure a smooth integration of the new executive in to his/her new role (applies to both external hires and internal promotions)

- failed to establish necessary critical skills, attributes or values such as team building skills, organizational ability, commitment, work ethic, technical expertise, advocacy skill, or any number of other necessary attributes.

- failed to understand the candidate's true strengths, weaknesses and proclivities and how they potentially influence the candidate's success and the organization as a whole

- made judgments and decisions too quickly, too emotionally, and placing too much emphasis on the resume, first impression, appearance, affability, articulation, or charisma

- made hiring decisions based solely on educational credentials and tended to hire "in his own image".

- thought that a candidate's primary attitudes, values and propensities could or would change

OR

THE NEW EXECUTIVE

- He/she was arrogant, thought he/she had all the answers, did not consult the team for possible ideas

- He/she was hired because of his/her sales prowess and we did need revenues however, in the process of focusing on sales he/she let the rest of the operation go

- He/she did not take the time to determine how we had gotten where we are and what we looked like when things were working well

- He/she did not seem to understand what drove the business; he/she was focused on acquisitions that did not make sense for the business.

- He/she alienated several members of the board, did not seem to understand the concerns of the board members

- He/she could not get a real grasp on the operations of the company. He/she was never in full realization of what changes in strategy affected the shop floor

- He/she did not understand enough about the business to know when the numbers were starting to go awry

- He/she could not get his/her team right, had two misfires in a row in the same Executive Vice President position, and the board lost confidence in his/her hiring ability

- He/she did not take responsibility for his/her own integration including selecting appropriate mentors

- He/she did not win the respect of his/her peers, subordinates, or the board

- He/she did not understand the importance of learning the dreams, goals, and objectives of his/her team members

- He/she had a command and control leadership style and could not gain consensus among any of our constituencies

- He/she failed to establish a go-to network for different answers and challenges within the organization

- He/she could not unite his/her troops; they were always confused about priorities so key performance metrics suffered

- He/she did not realize or did not admit that he/she was human, that mistakes are made, need to be acknowledged, and apologized for quickly

- He/she was not sensitive to the needs and goals of all the organization's stakeholders

- He/she achieved quick results, but could not sustain results because of his/her short term view

- He/she found the company's financial position was not as it had been represented

- He/she found the company was mired in the past and that the senior leaders were not receptive to change

- He was a very nice man and was well liked, but he just could not move the numbers

- He/she was very strong in many areas, but not the areas that would help us

- He/she was not honest; he would always offer bull____ answers to questions to which he/she did not really have the answers, when he/she should have been honest and said he did not know

- He/she was really just kind of lazy. This is a hard charging organization. He/she was really smart but would not do what it took to get the job done when it required extra effort

- He/she had a cavalier attitude toward almost everything

- He/she could not articulate a clear vision and motivate the troops to move in his/her direction; he/she kept talking about the way his/her old company did things.

- He/she was not the kind of coach the organization needed. The company has grown so fast that we have a bunch of inexperienced people who need a lot of teaching and coaching

- He/she had a style that was incompatible with the company and it turned out to be a big issue. This is a very formal buttoned-down organization and he/she was very informal and laid back. The customers did not relate to him/her

- He/she was not a quick study. One has to learn quickly around here. Nobody is spoon-fed.

- He/she could not solve problems or conflicts. When he/she found himself/herself under pressure he/she would simply yell at others.

- He/she seemed to be much too quick to assign blame, seldom accepting responsibility

- He/she got bogged down in the details and never could see the forest for the trees.

Between 45 percent and 50 percent of all executive hires fail within eighteen months. Of the 3,033 failed CEO and executive level placements our firm examined, over 90 percent of those failures fall in to these categories:

HIRING FAILURE

- Poor Fit - The new CEO had been promoted beyond his or her level of competence. There was nothing in the candidate's background, experience, references and/or credentials that supported the candidate's ability to do the specific job or the business model may have changed. Pay close attention to the phase in which the company is operating: startup, growth, turnaround, etc.

- Poor Fit - The new CEO was misled or inadequately informed about the nature of the job, the condition of the company, the culture of the parent or stakeholder group or other material or critical success factors.

- Poor Fit - The new CEO may or may not have been experienced in building a leadership team well suited to carry out the organization's objectives.

EXECUTION FAILURE

- Failure - To objectively evaluate members of the leadership team. The new CEOs have tendency to want to replace key leaders before determining the best possible and prudent course of action. Less common, but still problematic, is a tendency to be overly loyal to the existing team.

- Failure - Not understanding the total operation including strategy, people and more commonly, operations. The new CEOs must become intimately familiar with the nuts and bolts operations of the business in order to be able to ask the right questions and know when the organization is on track and moving in the right direction

- Failure - Task oriented the opposite of the item above. The new CEOs that are particularly strong in one area, typically operations, ignore or minimize the big picture items.

- Failure - Lack of discipline. The new CEOs must quickly grasp the essence of the operation in order to establish strategic priorities. Poor discipline leads to growth strategies that do not make sense and failure to understand the true drivers of the business.

- Failure - To recognize the possibilities. The new CEO's lack of vision or emotional intelligence often causes them to become chained to an old business model or original vision, product line, marketing strategy, etc.

- Failure - To bond with the existing team. The new CEO's need to win the confidence of the existing team even if changes are eminent.

- Failure - To gel with members of the board. The new CEO's must have the confidence of the board members. Boards are comprised of individuals, each of whom have unique concerns and require an individual communications strategy. Board members must remain confident in the ability and willingness of the new CEO to make tough decisions with clarity and realism while communicating transparently and effectively with each board member.

There are other reasons that newly placed CEOs and senior executives fail. Eliminate these and you will most certainly stack the deck in your favor.

Unfortunately, reality is that in many cases where failure has been the outcome, there was nothing wrong with the candidate, the company, the hiring manager, or the opportunity.

The very best hiring practices examine as many variables as possible. While no process involving human beings can ever be perfect, the consultants in our firm seem to have broken the code when it comes to avoiding the most common hiring mistakes.

Many searches are destined for failure from the outset because many, if not most, of the important variables are neglected. Many searches are executed with little more than a "job description." The typical job description is nothing more than a list of attributes all based on background, experience and credentials, i.e. ten years of this, an MBA in that, et cetera. The job description is an important component of a comprehensive search specification. It does not, however, provide an adequate or appropriate roadmap for an effective search.

Getting it right is not always easy. Here is a quote out of Execunet's October 2007 e-newsletter:

There is mounting frustration with the pace of many executive search assignments, and these days, it's being voiced largely by executive recruiters who cannot seem to get enough organizational commitment to keep the momentum on search assignments.

Just consider the surge of responses to a question about why searches are getting stalled that came in from corporate hiring executives who count themselves among the members of ExecuNet's exclusive Human Resources Executive Business Roundtable.

One discussion contributor who just left a senior HR role confirms that the pace of executive search assignments has indeed been slowed by a variety of organizational pressures.

"The pace of activity inside companies is frantic. New fires develop every day that require immediate attention. Executives are overbooked and priorities are juggled. Their availability is limited. Executive recruiters find their calls going unreturned," says the longtime HR officer.

"Another factor is evolving job specifications," he says. "Senior executives frequently think they know what they want in a candidate, but their perspective changes as they react to resumes and initial interviews. From first-hand experience, what started as a search for one set of experiences turns into something only loosely associated with the initial specs." And no matter how stretched management may be, executives will apparently take whatever extra time they believe they need to select the perfect candidate.

We are mindful of the pressures hiring managers' face and are careful to be empathetic. This awareness is critical to developing and enhancing client relationships. This kind of empathy is also critical when working with clients and candidates at every stage of the search.

Every physician takes the Hippocratic Oath before he or she can graduate from medical school, become licensed and begin to practice medicine. Unfortunately, there is no such licensing or certification process for retained executive search professionals, nor is there any such mantra or sworn oath. In our judgment, there should be: MAKE NO ASSUMPTIONS. Every senior level search should start with a clean sheet of paper. Relying on the by-products of recently conducted similar searches in order to present yet another list of the usual suspects is a practice which should be avoided at all costs.

Remember that the "business as usual" approach to hiring CEOs and senior executives leaves much to be desired.

"Business as usual" questions in selecting search firms include:

- How many searches have you done in this industry?
- How many similar searches have you done during the last twelve months?
- What does your network look like in our industry?
- How many CEO searches have you conducted in our industry?

Brooke Masters wrote and published an article in the *Financial Times,* March 2009 edition highlighting the career of Kevin Kelly the CEO at Heidrick & Struggles. This is an excerpt from that article.

Since taking the helm in 2006, Mr. Kelly, 43, has sought to move the firm away from pure recruiting to offering a suite of services that help its clients attract, retain and promote top management. The work was sparked by a recent internal study of 20,000 Heidrick searches, he says.

"We've found that 40 percent of executives hired at the senior level are pushed out, fail or quit within 18 months. It's expensive in terms of lost revenue. It's expensive in terms of the individual's hiring. It's damaging to morale."

The most prestigious search firms in the world are typically strong proponents of asking these kinds of boilerplate questions, principally because they are prepared to answer them. I am not citing this article as a disparagement of this firm or any other; more as a suggestion that there might be a more meaningful set of questions to which you might want answers.

Questions like this suggest to me that the buyer might not have a full appreciation of exactly what it is they are seeking. It seems to my firm that the questions should be much more *outcome focused*. A set of more relevant questions might look like this:

1. What is the firm's successful delivery rate? Or what percentage of the firm's engagements is considered successful by the client?

2. Does the firm track its performance and/or retention rate?

3. What is the total number of searches the firm has conducted and over what period of time?

4. Is the firm accredited by the Association of Executive Search Consultants? (Less than 200 firms worldwide are certified by the AESC)

5. Does the firm conduct comprehensive primary research on every search or do they depend primarily on databases and informal networks?

6. What does the firm's needs-analysis process look like and what are the key discovery items it seeks to unearth or reveal?

7. Does the firm understand performance based search methodology?

8. How many personal contacts will be made and <u>who</u> *(Partner, senior associate or research assistant)* will make them?

9. How many of your competitors are off limits to the search firm as a result of their existing client relationships?

10. What kind of analyses or metrics will the firm measure potential candidates against?

11. Will the firm require its candidates to complete a self-appraisal?

12. How will the firm know that your opportunity is ideal for the candidates they select and present?

13. Does the firm utilize structured interviewing and <u>who</u> *(Partner, senior associate or research assistant)* will conduct the interviews?

14. Will the firm conduct just cursory reference checks or comprehensive 360's in advance of presentation, <u>who</u> *(Partner, senior associate or research assistant)* will conduct them, and what form will they take?

15. Will the firm be able to coach me on team fit and effectiveness?

16. Who conducts background investigations and in what manner?

17. How long will the search take?

18. Is the firm flexible, focused on me and willing to customize my search?

19. What is the total cost of the search including direct and indirect expenses?

20. Will the firm be capable of assisting me in the successful integration of the newly hired executive?

21. Will the firm provide me with meaningful market information collected while conducting my search?

I have thrown a lot of "stuff" at you to get you thinking. The failure rate among newly placed executives is alarming and it is getting worse. In my opinion, this trend is nothing short of a crisis. Every time one of these mis-fires occurs, a lot of bad things happen. The most obvious and most talked about is the loss of financial performance at the client site.

Somewhat less obvious is the disruption and/or loss of momentum within the client organization. The total cost of mis-hires and or mis-promotions has been estimated (depending on which study you read) at somewhere between 5 and 10 times the executive's annual compensation. Based on my real-world experiences, I believe the cost to be substantially greater.

Something that does not get talked about or lamented over nearly enough in my opinion, are the lives of candidates, spouses, children and family that are needlessly disrupted, sometimes permanently, as a result of poorly executed hiring processes.

The pages that follow contain suggestions that have worked for Allen Austin.

TWO

Needs Analysis

If you do not ask the right questions, the answers do not matter! Whether you choose to use a professional search firm or not, the steps taken should be the same. Do these things right the first time, and you will reap the rewards. Take short cuts and chances are roughly 50 percent your new hires will fail within eighteen months.

Keep in mind that this book is written from the perspective of a search consultant whose objective is to facilitate matches that work and last. For over thirty-five years, I have been making real-world observations of what works and what does not work. The recommendations I make are those I know to be effective.

The degree of success achieved as a result of any search will, in large part, be driven by the quality of questions asked and the quality of the answers provided by the hiring manager.

Every search should start by conducting a very thorough needs analysis, a process designed to discover exactly what it will take for a candidate to be successful in a specific role. Be mindful of specific elements in your environment that might indicate a good or bad fit for different candidates. For my firm and in the case of an existing client, the time required to conduct such an analysis can be as little as an hour or two. However, it has taken up to three days in the case of a new client with extremely complex challenges and multiple challenges.

The material that follows will give you a very good feel for how to conduct a needs analysis. The more you dig and the more you discipline yourself to fast forward the tape and think about how you will determine success for your new CEO or senior executive, the better the outcome of your search.

Please remember these are only examples. They are standard templates that can be customized for specific industries and functional positions. This approach to search and consulting is surgical, specific, customized, and focused. At Allen Austin, we start with a clean sheet of paper on each engagement; therefore, the examples I have provided may be more or less complex than the actual engagements requires.

EXAMPLE

Company/Organization

1. What are the most salient points we should know about the company's story?

2. What should we know about the company's mission, vision, strategy, and most current initiatives?

3. What are your growth plans for this year and beyond? How is the company performing compared to the plan?

4. What would you like to learn from the market that should be included in the 20-day market report?

Culture/Alignment

1. How would you describe your culture?

2. What makes your company a great place to work?

3. What kinds of behaviors are valued at your company?

4. What forces drive and most heavily influence your business (i.e., operations, finance, marketing, sales)?

5. What are the three most important values the ideal candidate share with you as an organization? How does your organization view humility?

6. How would you describe the style of leadership and execution at your company?

7. Are you interested in exploring executive team fit and alignment?

The Opportunity

1. What makes this position compelling?

2. What does this position offer that might compel an A player from your competition or best practices employer to want to jump ship?

3. How will this position grow? Will the opportunities be substantially different over time?

4. What is the nature of the team with whom this new executive will work?

Position Specific Performance

1. Please provide a complete top-to-bottom organizational chart, including specific responsibilities and headcount.

2. What are the ten most important, specific deliverables for this position? Please rank them in order.

3. Are there specific deadlines for this position?

4. How will this position grow? Will the objectives be substantially different over time?

5. What is the specific nature of the candidate's profit-and-loss responsibility, forecasting, line item, autonomy, budget approval, et cetera?

6. What political and/or organizational land mines or challenges will this person face?

7. Why is this position open? Who occupied the position previously? Did they meet expectations?

8. How will success be determined in this position, quantitatively and qualitatively?

9. How many direct reports are there? How many direct reports do you expect in a year from now? How large is the division's headcount/organization? How large do you expect it to be in a year?

10. Who are the top five people, internal or external, with whom the candidate will have the most interaction? Where are they located?

Background, Experience & Credential Requirements

1. What is the ideal background for this position (industry-specific experience, best practices, processes, functional, etc.)?

2. How important are industry contacts or an established network of some kind?

3. What are the educational requirements of this position?

4. What other core competencies can you think of that this candidate must possess?

5. Travel requirements: How often? To where? On average how long are the trips? Does it include attending any relevant industry events?

Interview Process

1. Is there any specific testing that you would like the firm to perform during the candidate sourcing/vetting process?

2. Please list who should receive the candidate packets. Do you require hard copies as well as electronic versions? Should everyone on the distribution list receive compensation information also?

3. Please list who will interview the candidates, including their role, and provide a short bio to be shared with the candidate.

4. What are you looking for in this person? When you conduct an interview, what key questions will you ask?

5. What is your interviewing process? How long does the process typically take?

6. Do you plan to interview everyone in your office?

7. If a candidate has to travel to you to interview, who will make the travel arrangements? Who will initially pay? Who will coordinate the candidate's travel?

8. Do you wish to conduct phone interviews first before a face-to-face interview?

9. Typically we receive feedback on each candidate interviewed over the phone or in person within twenty-four hours of the interview. Do you anticipate any problems with this request? Do you have an established procedure for debrief?

10. Please confirm who will handle background checks (criminal, verification of education, etc.).

Candidate Package Considerations

1. What benefits are to be included in the candidate's hiring package (e.g., compensation package, base, bonus, relocation package, points, realtor, lawyers, packing, moving, unpacking, animal transport, auto, house-hunting trip, car or car allowance)?

2. This year, we are experiencing unique challenges relating to the real estate and credit markets. What kinds of things should we try to anticipate (e.g., relocation, sale of residence, home-buying)?

THREE

Search Specification

The output of a quality needs analysis is a written search specification. Starting a senior level search without a well written document or roadmap is tantamount to building an office building without a set of plans. Now I know a guy who built a beautiful ten thousand square foot home near Johnson City, Texas without plans, or so he claimed. He also said that 90 percent of the materials for this structure, which doubled as a hunting lodge, came right off of his land. There are certainly exceptions to every rule, but you are clearly stacking the odds in your favor if you will discipline yourself to follow a proven process.

Our specification becomes the roadmap for each search, and it is always a joint venture between our client and our search consultant. Indeed, we do not start a search until we have executed a comprehensive needs analysis with the client's key decision makers, and are able to obtain a complete buy-in on the entire search process including the research piece and target list. Because we feel so strongly about this phase of the search, we do not accept every assignment we are offered. We do not accept assignments from employers who have demonstrated irresponsible employment practices, employers with unrealistic expectations or employers who are not willing to partner with Allen Austin. Great searches are seldom the result of the unilateral efforts of a search firm or its consultant. Great searches, more often than not, are the result of a collaborative effort between all key decision makers on the hiring side, and the lead search consultant on the search firm side.

In our judgment, an effective search specification contains a minimum of five key elements: a company positioning, opportunity positioning, job description, performance expectations and a description of living conditions in the area. If the needs-analysis has been conducted properly, most of the search spec work has already been done.

Remember one thing as it relates to the search specification. Unless we are talking about a confidential search, the search specification is the primary marketing piece for the search. Typically, this document will be read by many people who are potential candidates and many who are not. This document should do a great job "selling" the company, the opportunity and the physical location of the job.

Since the majority of candidates sourced for a particular situation will more than likely be happily and successfully employed, selling the opportunity is key. We believe strongly that the opportunity should be sold; not the candidate. Sell the opportunity and require the candidate to sell him or herself. Avoid the trap of selling candidates on making a move. If the search specification and the consultant involved have done a good job selling (not embellishing) the opportunity; the right candidates should draw their own conclusions without unnecessary pressure. It is this "selling" I am talking about which can indeed compromise the outcome of the search. Remember the objective should be to facilitate a match that works for you and candidate alike; not to force or cajole a square peg in to a round hole.

EXAMPLE

Next is an example of a well written search specification for Custom Metals & Pigments Inc., Managing Director – Americas.

The Company

Custom Metals & Pigments Inc. was founded in 1945 by aluminum industry pioneer Ernest Scheller, Sr. as Metals Powder, Inc. in Stamford, Connecticut. His vision was to create a business that would provide the highest quality products and customized service in a manner of unyielding integrity.

Custom Metals & Pigments Inc.
Corporate Headquarters
Hometown, Pennsylvania

Recognized today as a world leader in the manufacture and supply of aluminum effect pigments, Custom Metals & Pigments Inc. is that company envisioned by Ernest Scheller over 60 years ago. Still a family owned and led business with an extraordinary commitment to its employees; today's Custom Metals & Pigments Inc. is a $100 million plus operation with over 700 employees world-wide with manufacturing, technical and research centers in Europe, Asia and North America. Through highly experienced executive account managers, technical service representatives and a world-wide network of independent agents and distributors, Custom Metals & Pigments Inc. markets and services its products to a variety of end use markets including automotive, graphic arts and printing inks, plastics, and industrial coatings. Custom Metals & Pigments Inc.'s innovative special effect and performance-enhancing pigments add beauty and value to many products.

Looking toward the future, Custom Metals & Pigments Inc. is moving from its history as a ball-milling company to a special effects and performance pigments company. Custom Metals & Pigments Inc. is in the process of transforming itself from "metal mashers" to "Architects of Light®." Custom Metals & Pigments

Inc. is redefining itself through science.

Through the years, Custom Metals & Pigments Inc. has built a strong foundation based on its core values of:

- Business with integrity
- Customer Focus
- Commitment to employees
- Commitment to the community
- Commitment to safety – internal and external customers
- Commitment to the environment
- Commitment to continual improvement

With state of the art research, technical and manufacturing facilities in North America, Scotland, and Asia, Custom Metals & Pigments Inc. has set the standard for excellence in providing products that meet the needs of global customers who expect brilliant visual effects, excellent performance, expanded functional capabilities, and the highest quality products.

CUSTOM METALS & PIGMENTS INC.
MANAGING DIRECTOR—AMERICAS

The Opportunity

The next Managing Director – Americas will be a transformational, persuasive and organizationally savvy leader, capable of restoring the Americas business to a true leadership position in the industry. This is a rare opportunity for a proven general manager with a keen sense of global markets, world-class manufacturing processes and a history of driving sales and profits in new product-driven environments.

This opportunity is one of the most exciting we have seen. Custom Metals & Pigments Inc. is reinventing its business and as such is reinventing the market itself. With world-class technology and chemistry, a true transformation is underway. Formerly a milling company, Custom Metals & Pigments Inc. is quickly becoming a special effects company. Superlative scientists from all over the world have located to the global labs in Hometown, PA and the St. Andrews area in Scotland. They are now driving innovation and creation of brand new products. The global technology team, after only a year in place, is bringing products never before seen in the international marketplace.

The Managing Director - Americas position is a hands-on role, requiring energy and enthusiasm to lead impactful change while reinforcing the values of the family. It is a sterling opportunity to lead and mold the company's largest business unit, to interact with global counterparts to create a worldwide enterprise and to have a dramatic impact on the direction and results of this fundamentally strong organization. The successful candidate will be able to leverage best practices to produce new products and capitalize on synergies throughout the global organization, while at the same time, be able to focus on the details and drive engineering projects and change initiatives. Intimate contact with important customers will be key to capitalizing on the new manufacturing and technology prowess.

Our client is most interested in candidates who bring a firm grasp of general business principles, strategy, manufacturing and commercial operations on a global scale. Success as the Managing Director – Americas will position the candidate for COO or CEO responsibility within five years.

CUSTOM METALS & PIGMENTS INC.
MANAGING DIRECTOR—AMERICAS

The Position

The global organization of Custom Metals & Pigments Inc. includes a CEO, a COO and three operating divisions: The Americas, Europe and Asia-Pacific. The Americas is the largest of the three divisions. Each of the Managing Directors for the three divisions reports to the COO. The Managing Director - Americas position is currently vacant. It is the subject of this executive search.

Reporting directly to the Managing Director – Americas are the following regional organizations: Sales, Marketing, Engineering, Manufacturing, Supply Chain and Human Resources. Additionally, the Global Marketing Director for Automotive reports directly to the Managing Director – Americas. The corporate CFO reports to the CEO and COO, while the Controller – Americas reports to the Managing Director-Americas on a dotted line. All other functions are corporate in-nature.

Over the last three years, the sales and profits of The Americas operation have declined markedly, primarily due to Custom Metals & Pigments Inc.'s dependence upon sales of product to the Big Three American automakers (and their suppliers). The global recession of the last 18 months and its impact on all product sales have exacerbated the downturn for Custom Metals & Pigments Inc. in The Americas. This is a true turnaround situation.

Candidate Profile

The successful candidate for the Managing Director-Americas position must be:
- A proven leader, with hands-on experience in a turnaround situation
- Capable of working in a privately-held, family-owned company, quickly recognizing and adapting to the unique cultural environment
- A driven change-agent, able to represent The Americas organization, while working very closely with other members of the Global Operating Board
- Able to effectively assess organizational strengths and weaknesses and to act upon his/her findings
- Qualified to quickly impact the bottom line of The Americas organization while developing the necessary skills to assume greater responsibilities within the organization

Professional Experience

The ideal candidate will have the following education, experience and skills:

- Bachelor's degree in a technical field (engineering, chemistry etc.)
- Eight to ten years of progressively responsible experience in an executive leadership position in a global operation
- Five years of managerial experience in a manufacturing environment
- Five years of experience leading a commercial organization
- Proven track record of leading an organization to sales and profit growth
- Demonstrated understanding and experience implementing modern manufacturing methodologies such as 6-Sigma or the Toyota Production System
- Demonstrated experience in consolidating enterprises to balance manufacturing and sales
- Strong understanding of financial management (Profit & Loss, Balance Sheet, Key Metrics, Activity Based Costing, Non-Cash Items)
- Strong personal presence with the ability to be the face of the organization and deliver impactful presentations to a variety of audiences
- A bias for safety and implanting and maintaining safe operations

The superior candidate will have all of the above, plus the following education, experience and skills:

- A Master's degree or higher in business, management or marketing. Any combination of technical and business related degrees is acceptable.
- Five additional years of progressively responsible experience in an executive leadership position.
- Recent experience as the General Manager/Business Unit President of an enterprise that includes multi-unit manufacturing operations
- Experience working in a unionized environment

- Knowledge of pigments and paste
- Knowledge of the automotive and related markets

Personal Attributes

integrity... to listen, learn, talk and teach... ability to question the status quo... highly motivated... visible... team player... strong leader... negotiator... strong backbone... focused... approachable... highly accountable and expect same... transformational leader... sense of urgency... not ego driven... big company perspective... global mindset...leads with humility...process oriented... relationship builder... superior intelligence... passion... personality... instills pride... active listener... decisive... speed with finesse... emotionally mature... curious... team builder

Performance Expectations – First 12 Months

- Restore profitability to The Americas business unit
- Re-establish the confidence of key customers in Custom Metals & Pigments Inc.'s capabilities
- Actively participate in a global rationalization of Custom Metals & Pigments Inc.'s sales and manufacturing bases, creating an urgency for resolution consistent with the economic realities
- Together with the R&D organization, identify product needs in the market that match Silberline's core competencies and new product capabilities
- Right-size The Americas' organization in line with anticipated business conditions

The Community

The Corporate Headquarters of Custom Metals & Pigments Inc. and the home base of the Managing Director – Americas is located in Hometown, Pennsylvania. The closest suburban area is the Lehigh Valley which is an easy and scenic drive from Hometown. The majority of the senior management at Custom Metals & Pigments Inc. commutes from the Lehigh Valley. The Lehigh Valley region of eastern Pennsylvania is made up of Lehigh and Northampton Counties and is home to the three cities of Allentown, Bethlehem and Easton, as well as numerous townships and boroughs. With more than half-a-million residents, it is the third largest metro region in the state.

Located less than two hours from New York, the Pocono Mountains and the New Jersey shore and an hour from Philadelphia, Lehigh Valley's metropolitan lifestyle is equally balanced by its outdoor offerings. There is country flair to the area that brings residents and visitors alike into the great outdoors.

Allentown, Pennsylvania

Lehigh Valley's 730 square miles of rolling hills offer immense options for business and pleasure. Popular attractions include art museums and galleries, sporting events and historical sites. Rural countryside vistas are available in a short drive outside the cities. These rural areas are home to wineries, outdoor activities, skiing, zoos and walking, hiking and biking trails.

Lehigh Valley is so named because it comprises an actual valley that lies between two large Pennsylvania mountain ranges, Blue

Mountain to the north and South Mountain to the south.

The Lehigh Valley has four distinct seasons, which typically include humid summers, cold winters, and very short and mild springs and falls. The area's warmest month (on average) is July at 84 °F (29 °C) and the coldest month (on average) being January at 35 °F (2 °C). The average precipitation of the area is 45.17 inches (1,147 mm) per year.

Housing

When it comes to housing, the Lehigh Valley is definitely one of the best places in the East to make a home. The region offers a much lower cost of living than most other Northeastern regions with easy access to major cities. The price is definitely right when it comes to making a home in the Lehigh Valley. The cost of living in the Lehigh Valley is less than New York City and Boston metro areas. Personal income and property taxes are also very favorable. Housing options run the gamut from beautiful historic homes to modern new construction. New residents can choose a place that provides quiet country living or go for the convenience of a city neighborhood.

Education

With eleven colleges and universities, a wealth of top-notch public and private schools for K-12 students and numerous career training programs, the Lehigh Valley goes right to the head of the class when it comes to education.

K-12: Approximately 83,000 students attend public schools in the Lehigh Valley, while others opt for private and parochial educations. There are 17 public school districts and numerous top-quality private schools in the area. More than 4,000 students attend the area's state-of-the-art secondary vocational and technical schools.

Higher Education: More than 45,000 students attend eleven area colleges and universities including Penn State University – Lehigh

Valley Campus, Lehigh University, DeSales University, East Stroudsburg University and Kutztown University.

Healthcare

Not only is the Lehigh Valley home to nationally recognized hospitals, but it also enjoys innovative health education services, numerous alternative healthcare providers and a wide selection of health and fitness facilities. The Lehigh Valley's hospitals are among the best in the nation. The Lehigh Valley Hospital & Health Network is considered one of the nation's finest regional hospitals. In 2003, Lehigh Valley Hospitals' three hospitals, two in Allentown and one in Bethlehem were honored to receive the prized National Quality Health Care award, presented by the National Committee for Quality in Health Care, based in Washington, D.C. In the same year, U.S. News ranked Lehigh Valley Hospital & Health Network highest in the region for heart care and heart surgery. The St. Luke's Hospital & Health Network is the only area hospital to have ever been named as one of the 100 top hospitals in the United States.

Application

Custom Metals & Pigments Inc. has engaged Allen Austin Global Executive Search to conduct the search for its next Managing Director—Americas. Interested candidates should submit a resume and cover letter to:

Rob Andrews
Allen Austin Global Executive Search
4345 Post Oak Place Drive, Suite 217
Houston, Texas 77027

FOUR

The Opportunity

By comparison, yesterday's "talent wars" appear little more than a friendly playground scuffle. In other words, if you think finding and retaining talent has been difficult in the recent past ... you ain't seen nothing yet!

What can you do about it? Unless you want to be drowned by the metaphorical wall of water that is bearing down on us, doing nothing or living with processes that need fixing makes little sense. In that meaningful action is invariably the by-product of a well thought through question; considering the following is probably a good place to start.

1. *Can you put your hand on your heart and say that your organization's hiring process is absolutely best-in-class? Note: if the individual responsible for talent management is not a part of the top team, you have work to do.*

2. *It is the quality of your organization's story that attracts talent; does your firm have a compelling story? If a candidate meets several people during the hiring process, do they all share the same story? No less important, is the story complemented by speed of action throughout the hiring process?*

3. *Are all those involved in the hiring process fully trained in behavioral interviewing? If not, when will that training start?*

4. *Is the business currently looking for talent in places you have not looked before? And if so, where?*

5. *Does your organization see leadership development as a business imperative? How could today's approach be taken to the next level?*

6. *Is coaching a way of life in your organization? Are you personally a masterful coach?*

7. *Does your firm provide an opportunity for employees at all levels to enter into an open and action-laden conversation about what they need from the organization? Note: this means going well beyond the typical engagement questionnaire. It is ironic that much of the work referred to as "engagement" does not actually engage employees.*

8. *Are you striving to make your own team's work experience more fulfilling? Simplifying processes, enriching and enlarging jobs, facilitating movement between roles, and increasing employment flexibility should take center stage.*

These questions will hopefully kick-start initial actions, but should not be considered anything like a complete list. We know that people are attracted to an organization by the vibrancy of its story, and that people leave when they feel they are not valued. Other aspects of the attraction/retention equation include a sense of personal growth, knowing what is going on, role fit, challenging work, the freedom to act, being part of a successful team, feeling that the pay is fair, the quality of leadership inside the business, regular feedback, the reputation of the product and/or service provided, and something that is often forgotten: people want to work for an organization that cares. When all is said and done, however, the single most powerful retention tool in any leader's behavioral arsenal is simply catching 'em doing it right!

As a final thought and daunting as the prospect might be, when we look back five years from now, from a talent management perspective, the evidence suggests we will describe today as "the good old days." This is an excerpt from John O. Burdett's article entitled *The Perfect Storm.*

EXAMPLE 1

This is a newly created position with VPS. Given the company's aggressive growth plan and management's desire to transition in to Generation Two Leadership, this is a tremendous opportunity for the right individual to build and lead an organization toward world-class status in a sector where no such player exists.

This person will also be considered to replace the incumbent chief executive officer upon his retirement. The vice president client support will be very visible in the supermarket community and will have an opportunity to build life-long relationships among the industry's leadership.

This is a superb opportunity for a consummate leader with a passion for success within the supermarket industry and at the retail unit level. For those who tend to reject big company constraints, politics and limitations in favor of a smaller, faster more nimble organization dedicated to integrity, professionalism, respect, exceeding client expectations, win-win relationships, and doing the next right thing. It will also be attractive to those who enjoy working a good part of their time with their clients in the day-to-day retail environment.

EXAMPLE 2

The next CEO of Woodland Blinds will be a transformational leader responsible for moving the company to the next phase in its evolution. The CEO's primary mission will include developing strategic sales & marketing plans and establishing the sales organization to implement it. This is an ideal position for a consummate leader and general manager with a penchant for sales and marketing.

This is a hands-on function, requiring the energy and enthusiasm to deal with the mundane and the intellect and imagination to work in the abstract.....an opportunity to have ongoing meaningful impact on the direction and results of the company.

The successful candidate will be entrepreneurial by nature, with a participative management and leadership style and will take an aggressive approach to the growth and development of the company. The next CEO will be capable of developing strategies to successfully launch new products, identify and develop new sales channels while expanding the existing channels, and broaden the customer base. Good general business judgment, not just financial acumen will be essential for success.

Our client is most interested in candidates who bring a firm grasp of general business principles, strategy, and complete knowledge of manufacturing practices where labor intensity is the norm. The CEO must possess the ability to command respect through presence, business knowledge, and a practical understanding of the business.

Remember that I am recommending that you do everything in your power to sell your opportunity and not the candidate. Most job or opportunity descriptions fail to answer the "so what?" question; which is why I should consider leaving my cushy position at your biggest competitor to come join you.

At the end of the day, you are looking for a leader who fits. You are looking for a leader who wants to be a part of what you are doing. You are looking for a leader ready, willing, and able to take you where you want to go. You are looking for a leader who shares your values, your attitudes, and has career aspirations in alignment with your plan. You are trying to fill your slot with the very best A Player available and potentially interested in your opportunity, for all of the right reasons.

Without a compelling opportunity statement, you are depending on compensation to lure your next CEO. If compensation is your only vehicle for recruiting at this level, you will almost certainly attract the very best of the displaced, underperforming, and disgruntled.

FIVE

Your Employment Brand

Whether you know it or not, your organization already has an employment brand. If you have already developed your formal employment brand, you are ahead of most. If you have not, now is the time to start. Here are a few examples taken from the "2009 list of Best Companies to Work For" to get you thinking:

1. **NetApp**

   At NetApp we pride ourselves on our innovation and creating an environment where people can make a difference. We embrace creativity, risk taking and continuous improvement. Our company culture is defined by our core values - trust and integrity, leadership, simplicity, teamwork and synergy, going beyond, to get things done - these aspirations are at the heart of NetApp. A key differentiator for NetApp is that our employees live these values every day. These values are the strength and foundation of our culture.

2. **Edward Jones**

   At Edward Jones, we're guided by a set of long-standing principles. We serve individual investors, like you. We opt for proven, long-term investing strategies instead of the latest investment fads. And, while we share information on our Web site, we believe it's more important to provide personalized attention and build relationships face to face in our local, community-based offices. Our firm was built on a foundation of principles that help guide us every day.

Take a look at how these principles guide our investment decisions and client relationships. Our financial advisors make every effort to build one-on-one relationships with clients, offering personalized attention and financial guidance

3. Boston Consulting Group

We partner with our clients to deliver customized solutions that resolve their most significant issues and create lasting competitive advantage. Utilizing decades of industry experience and functional expertise, BCG looks beyond standard solutions to develop new insights, mobilize organizations, drive tangible results, and make companies more capable. We seek to be agents of change for our clients, our people, and society broadly.

4. Google

At Google, we understand that our worldwide success results from our globally diverse workforce. In every Google office, you will find challenging projects and smart people with potential to change the world. Googler's relish the freedom to create the next generation of web technologies in an environment designed to foster collaboration, creativity, health, and happiness. Google is not a conventional company and we do not intend to become one. True, we share attributes with the world's most successful organizations a focus on innovation and smart business practices comes to mind but even as we continue to grow, we're committed to retaining a small-company feel. At Google, we know that every employee has something important to say, and that every employee is integral to our success. We provide individually-tailored compensation packages that can be comprised of competitive salary, bonus, and equity components, along with the opportunity to earn further financial bonuses and rewards.

5. Wegman's Food Market

At Wegman's, we believe that good people, working toward a common goal, can accomplish anything they set out to do. We care about the well-being and success of every person. High standards are a way of life. We pursue excellence in everything we do. We make a difference in every community we serve. We respect and listen to our people. We empower our people to make decisions that improve their work and benefit our customers and our company.

6. Cisco Systems

At Cisco customers come first and an integral part of our DNA is creating long-lasting customer partnerships and working with them to identify their needs and provide solutions that support their success. The concept of solutions being driven to address specific customer challenges has been with Cisco since its inception.

7. Genentech

Our employees cite the chance to make a difference in the lives of patients as the number one reason they enjoy working at Genentech. In hiring new employees, we look for people who are inspired by this mission and who would fit in well with the collaborative, rigorous and entrepreneurial spirit of the company culture. Because we know that employees are critical to our success in bringing novel medicines to patients, we are dedicated to remaining a great place to work and to providing employees with programs, services and benefits that allow them to bring the best to the business and to their personal lives.

8. Methodist Hospital System

The Methodist Hospital is a place where your compassion gives comfort, your talent drives innovation, and your care makes a difference. Our mission is to provide high quality, cost-effective health care that delivers the best value to the people we serve in a spiritual environment of caring in association with internationally recognized teaching and research.

9. Goldman Sachs

Our primary responsibility is clear to succeed on our clients' behalf. We constantly strive to anticipate our clients' rapidly changing needs and to develop new services to meet them. We stress creativity and imagination in everything we do, and always look for a better solution to a client's problem. People create success, which is why we go to great lengths to attract, inspire and reward creativity and talent. As a global business, our people come from all over the world and represent different nationalities, educational backgrounds and life experiences. We welcome their unique perspectives, their energy and ideas and their willingness to learn as well as to teach. A commitment to integrity, team work and the pursuit of excellence is at the core of everything we do. As with so many who have come before us, we believe you will find at Goldman Sachs some of the richest opportunities and most interesting challenges of your life.

10. Nugget Market

At Nugget, nothing is as important to us as quality, (except maybe exceptional guest service, low prices, and huge selection). Ok, so a lot of things are important to us here. It does not matter if it's our produce, our meats, our deli foods or our grocery products. If it's not the highest quality, it does not belong in our stores. That's one reason for our almost unreasonably lenient return policy. If you're not happy with a product you purchase in our stores, simply bring it back, and we will replace it or give you a full refund, no questions asked. We hope our guests never have to use this policy, but we're happy to provide it.

Today's candidates rank brand as the second most influential factor when deciding whether to accept an offer.

Just five years ago, less than one in ten Fortune 200 companies had a dedicated role to manage the employment brand, yet today more than 25 percent of Fortune 200 companies have dedicated headcount and budget to the practice.

Employment branding is the practice of managing your firm's image or reputation as an excellent place to work. Because so many factors influence how an organization is perceived, employment branding is loosely defined, yet must be addressed in today's world.

If you have not sufficiently answered the question: What is it about my company that will cause A-Players to jump ship and come to work for me? You have work to do.

SIX

Your Company's Story

When competition for top talent is intense, and when there seems to be a glut of available talent, your company's story is important. People stay with organizations they want to be a part of.

Talk about your company's mission, vision, strategy and most current initiatives and do not just cut and paste the stuff off of your website. Most of the time those words are not current and do not stir anyone's soul.

I conducted about three dozen searches for the supercenter division of Kmart between 1994 and 1996. This was a very tumultuous time for Kmart. Stock value was at an all time low, Joe Antonini was being forced out as chief executive and the mere mention of the word Kmart would usually get a recruiter a dial tone in response.

We were very successful recruiting an extremely talented and motivated team because we were able to carefully articulate Ron Floto, the new division president's strategy, growth and tactical plans. The vision of the new leadership team was what motivated some of the top retailing professionals in the food industry at that time to leave their current employers to join a team with a bold vision.

I should also add that Ron Floto's strategy turned out to be very effective, producing a $150 million bottom line turnaround. Unfortunately, the corporation ultimately lost focus on the supercenter concept and folded it back in to the general population.

When developing your story for purposes of recruiting, tell the whole story and not just the good parts. If your strategy is working, say so. If your results are not what you had planned, say so. It is only through articulating exactly where you are, and where you want to go that you will be able to identify and attract the ideal candidate(s).

Here are a couple of examples:

EXAMPLE 1

Founded in 1936, Smith's is the nation's seventeenth largest food retailer, operating approximately 175 stores with revenues of approximately $4.7 billion. The company currently operates two different store formats, 145 are combo stores while 45 are classified superstores.

With revenues approaching $40 million per store, Smith's is one of the largest volume operators in the industry. The company is headquartered in Your City, California. Smith's primary competitors are A&P, Safeway, Shopper's Food, and Kroger. The company has, for some time, operated an in-house ad agency.

Smith's is currently slightly ahead of plan on our very aggressive strategy set in place at the end of 2006. We are outperforming the competition by a wide margin.

Unknown to most, Smith's is in the process of developing some of the most innovative concepts in the industry. We are developing a totally new shopping format focused on the ever more prevalent dual income family. Included in our new format stores will be large prepared food centers, meals to go centers, ingredients ready to cook centers, phone in order processing, and more. Smith's is also focused on a top secret market niche currently unoccupied by any food retailer in the western United States. We are projecting retrofit sales performance of +25 percent - 25 percent combined with 3-5 percentage point gross margin improvement.

Backed by $2.5 million of solid consumer research our mission with these new concept stores is to become THE destination store for the consumer seeking the most attractive total value proposition. Our growth plans for the near future include 25 new stores and 50 remodels per year for the next four years until the entire store base is either new or remodeled.

EXAMPLE 2

For more than thirty years, VPS has helped independent grocers succeed by transforming historic accounting activities into timely, accurate decision support tools. Headquartered in Baltimore, Maryland, with offices in Pittsburgh, Pennsylvania and Nashville, Tennessee, VPS currently serves approximately 270 operators representing approximately 1,800 supermarkets throughout the U.S.

Since its inception, VPS' core services have been built around providing independent retail grocers with the financial information needed to make informed operational decisions on a daily basis. VPS now provides accounting and payroll outsourcing, financial software applications and services, treasury management, payroll/human resources, shrink control & labor scheduling applications.

VPS' team of professionals has over three decades of retail grocery experience and they are developing solutions that are designed specifically for the retail grocery industry. VPS is considered to be the industry expert in benchmarking, best practices, and mission-critical support. VPS is the preferred provider of these services as endorsed by the National Grocer's Association.

VPS is rapidly becoming recognized as the go-to firm for best practices, benchmarking, and decision support in the independent supermarket community. The firm's vice president client experience management is becoming an icon in the industry as he delivers talks and white papers relevant to today's independent supermarket operator. VPS is proactive and visible in its efforts to educate the supermarket sector. Typically VPS has new clients approach them after having learned of VPS' prowess and having experienced some significant change event. VPS' revenues have doubled over the last four years and the company is experiencing a groundswell of newly interested potential clients. VPS has built the systems and processes that work and is now endeavoring to build out the human capital infrastructure to support them.

VPS is a dynamically growing ESOP company. 95 percent of VPS' revenues are recurring income from existing clients. VPS employs approximately fifty professionals and is in a progressive growth mode. Revenues have doubled over the last four years. VPS' overall strategy is to continue to add maximum value to its retail customers while continuing to build the company's ESOP value.

VPS is described as a "nice place to work." Employees at all levels are free and encouraged to voice their opinions and offer suggestions. Empowerment is a catch phrase in some organizations, but not here. Operating as a true ESOP company, VPS authority and autonomy to spend up to $5,000 in order to exceed customer expectations extends to the lowest level employee. The "command and control" mentality simply does not exist at VPS. The primary strategy at VPS is working very well. The company's opportunities lie in capitalizing on synergies and best practices in a much more meaningful way.

These examples are more compelling than the vast majority I see in search specifications floating around. While your company may not be undergoing these kinds of monumental changes, you should be able to articulate elements and attributes of your company that make it attractive.

SEVEN

Focus on Values

Focus on values. Now this is not something you can do overnight or by some marketing slogan or with smoke and mirrors. Be very aware however that clearly stated values are a very big deal.

Executive hires go awry when the values of the organization and those of the candidate are not in alignment. This is not about good and bad, right or wrong. As we say, it is about fit. Example: Virtually 100 percent of organizations say they have a focus on customers, yet very few really do.

An organization with whom I am intimately familiar, Pappas Brothers Restaurants, for many years gave incredible customer service by, among other things, giving all of their front line employees the authority and autonomy to "comp" an entire meal if the service was not up to the customer's expectations. This kind of extreme customer service demonstrated Pappas Brothers values as it relates to customer service. Chances are excellent that a manager who fits well in this environment would feel out of alignment in an organization where customer service is given lip service and all customer interactions are driven by company policy.

Once again, this is not about right or wrong, good or bad; some organizations value innovation, some do not. Some companies value creativity and risk taking, while others expect their leaders to be good soldiers; executors of a strategy driven from the top. Be very clear about who you are and what kind of individual you seek.

Findings from the 2009 BlueSteps Executive Mobility Survey show that, despite the current economic climate, 75 percent of currently employed executives are likely or very likely to consider a new job opportunity. As the global economy works toward recovery, executive level candidates are open to change and likely to consider new career development opportunities.

57 percent of executives surveyed expect to work for 4-7 organizations by the end of their career, and 48 percent say that 2 years is the shortest tenure an executive can have at an organization without compromising the value of one's resume. These results are comparable to data from the 2007 report.

When deciding to leave their current employer, "Poor company values" was cited as the most important factor in an executive's decision to leave his or her current employer, with 74 percent of respondents rating this as extremely important, up from 64 percent in 2007. "Poor company values" replaced "lack of career development" as executives' most pressing concern when deciding to leave a company; 63 percent of executives voted "lack of career development" as extremely important in 2009, down from 74 percent in 2007.

Remember that this is not about right or wrong. Some companies are focused on products with little focus on customers. Some companies are passionate about their intense work ethic and the fact their executives work six day work weeks. Values for purposes of alignment are neither bad nor good. They are what they are. Unless you are able to articulate your real values, you are likely to wind up with a CEO or senior executive who does not want to sail on your boat.

EIGHT

Focus on Culture

Focus on culture is critical for proper alignment of executive and organization. Culture is a tricky thing because the culture of an organization is rarely perceived the same at the rank and file level as it is in the executive suite.

What would your front line employees say about what is valued most at your company? Is it service, innovation, product design, execution, operations or price?

What drives your business? Do consumers, businesses, government entities, subsidies or contributors drive your company? It is amazing to me how many CEOs do not really understand what drives their companies.

What internal forces drive your company? Often overlooked, no company is ever perfectly balanced in terms of the influence and power wielded by the departments. Some companies are predominately driven by operations, some by marketing, some by finance, some by product development and the list goes on. It is not uncommon to see dissatisfaction on the part of a newly placed executive when he or she discovers that the department, division or business unit does not enjoy the same organizational clout expected.

What behavior(s) would your middle managers say is rewarded at you company? Now this is huge because the behavior that is revered in one company will get you fired in another. In some organizations, extremely competitive, bordering on predatory behavior is rewarded and encouraged. This kind of behavior may or may not be acceptable in your organization. While we never find these kinds of subtleties discussed on company websites, brochures, annual reports or in employee manuals, they are absolutely a reality and you need to come to grips with this issue in your organization. This is not about right or wrong, rather understanding reality and recognizing that a very fine executive who has flourished as a chief operating officer in one company may fail in another seemingly identical company, while holding a seemingly identical position.

What would your average two year employee say makes your company a good company to work for? These questions can lead to meaningful dialogue around culture and what types of individuals tend to do well in a particular environment. It will also be critically important that culture at executive level be addressed.

Develop a clear description of how the organization works, what kinds of behavior, contribution and interaction are valued, and how the organization tends to judge new hires. Is the organization accepting of newcomers? Are you receptive to new ideas, or are you steeped in the past?

There is no such thing as knowing too much about the culture of the organization in which you are about to place a new executive. Do not make the mistake we have seen many times: placing a well qualified executive who looks absolutely perfect on paper into an organization with cultural norms and values incompatible with those of the candidate. Remember a mature leopard is incapable of changing his spots! Also, do not assume that just because the placement occurs as a result of an internal promotion that the culture nuances are any less important. Each level within an organization has its own sub culture complete with its own set of land mines that have to be navigated.

Most organizations have what I call an execution style. Some have referred to it as the speed of the company. Some companies are very fast and some are painstakingly slow. Much of this is driven by the nature of the board of directors and the ownership structure. Some new CEOs are frustrated at the speed (or lack thereof) at which the board will allow them to make significant changes in the organization.

Do not forget about work ethic. Once again, no right or wrong here, let's just flush out the real picture. It would be an enormous mistake to bring a new executive, including a CEO, where work ethic compatibility was not explored.

EXAMPLE

In 2008, I met a very talented female executive who had moved her family to the U.S. from The Netherlands to assume the role of CFO in a $90 million power generation company. She lasted less than six months. This was a classic mismatch. Upon close examination, there was absolutely nothing wrong with the company, job, or candidate, just a huge mismatch. The CEO in this organization was a hard charging start-up CEO who worked eighty hours per week and required the same of his lieutenants. For many this would not have been a problem because there was a big pot of gold at the end of this start-up rainbow. After the fact, when the placement had fallen apart, the search consultant in charge of the search admitted that she knew there was a potential problem with her candidate. The candidate had made it clear that she placed work-life balance near the top of her list. The consultant was under such enormous pressure to complete the search that she chose to ignore a reality that had predestined the placement for failure.

EXAMPLE (SURVEY)

The following survey questions explore culture in your organization. In particular, the questionnaire explores two critical questions: How strong is your culture? To what extent does your culture support organizational agility? The underlying assumption - supported by research - is that in a fluid and rapidly-changing business environment both clarity and flexibility are demanded. Go through each of the questions and answer not with the way you want your organization to be, but as it is now. Ask respondents to answer on a scale of 1 – 10, with 10 meaning "Absolutely Yes".

Answer every question. Your response will, ideally, embrace the whole organization. If you are new to the organization, or part of a very large enterprise where you only get to see part of what happens, base your answers on the part of the organization you know well.

1. The organization's mission/purpose is absolutely clear

2. The organization's mission/purpose makes me feel that my job is important, and I'm proud to be part of this organization

3. We move faster than the competition when launching new products and service

4. As an organization we are quick to identify even subdue changes in the way the market place is unfolding

5. As a business we have an outstanding track record of anticipating and successfully responding to initiatives generated by the competition

6. Speed and simplicity are alive and well in everything we do

7. As a business I know we are measuring the right things

8. We excel at measuring effectiveness through the eyes of the customer, across the organization

9. I fully understand my role, what is expected of me today, and how and where I need to grow to succeed tomorrow

10. Honest and regular feedback is a way of life. That feedback draws on the specific competencies (behaviors) that describe success in my role

11. We are passionate in the way we live our organization's values. Our values shape our priorities and dominate decisions at every level of the organization

12. People around here feel that their concerns are both listened to and, whenever possible, addressed

13. Those who deliver results, but do not consistently live our values are confronted and, if necessary, separated from the organization regardless of level

14. People around here understand with great clarity the priorities that underscore their role

15. People around here who do not meet the agreed goals/results are held accountable regardless of level

16. The top team excels in building commitment to the vision

17. As a business we consistently learn from our mistakes

18. My team leader is both committed to, and skilled in, the way he/she supports my personal growth and development

19. The standards against which quality is judged (service, products, and processes) are absolutely clear across the business

20. Exploring new processes and innovative tools to better understand the customer's emerging needs is an ingrained discipline in this organization

21. Consistently challenging the established way of doing things is central to our culture

22. In the past three Mondays, I have had at least one meaningful discussion about my career

23. Positive reinforcement for good work is an ingrained habit around here

24. It would be fair to say that people around here have considerable freedom to act

25. Courageous conversation (candor) is a way of life. When we get together we regularly discuss "the un-discussable"

26. The organization's structure is designed to meet the need to "act fast." As a result stripping away unnecessary rules and bureaucracy is an ongoing process

27. Pushing the boundaries, taking risks, letting go of the past and being willing to explore uncharted territory is a natural part of the way the organization functions

28. We hear about it before it is in the press

29. Celebrating success is woven into the fabric of the business

30. You cannot get ahead around here unless you live and breathe "collaboration"

31. Everyone at the top gives a clear and consistent message about where we are heading and why

32. When a leader joins the organization, the tools and processes are in place to ensure he/she hits the ground running

33. Employees at every level "live" our brand (i.e., the promise implicit in the way we present our products/service to the marketplace)

34. We constantly seek better ways to bring the customers voice to internal meetings and critical decisions

35. Employees at every level buy in to, and are committed to, the organization's journey

36. Employees at every level understand why, where, and the speed at which we have to bring about change

A word of caution: I think surveys are a wonderful tool as a part of a comprehensive culture management strategy. Do not even consider conducting a survey of any of your organization unless you are fully committed to a series of appropriate responses to the survey results. Conducting a survey will stir the pot. Do not stir it unless you are willing to adjust the ingredients.

NINE

Specific Responsibilities

Carefully determine specific responsibilities and management skills necessary for success in the position. Remember management and leadership are two different disciplines. *It is possible to be a great manager and a lousy leader.* Management has to do with coping with complexity and order. Leadership has more to do with coping with ambiguity and change. Identify specific management skills necessary for the candidate to succeed not only today, but in the foreseeable future. Remember that no candidate is perfect and no one possesses every conceivable management skill.

Management skills basically have to do with planning, organizing, directing and controlling. Other things you should consider are problem identification and solving skills, process orientation, execution, follow through and resource allocation.

I have seen more than a few mismatches occur because the CEO or senior executive in question, while having excellent overall leadership attributes, did not have the ability to operate in a specific environment.

Example: An extremely effective supermarket CEO, who had exceeded shareholder expectations in a privately held debt free company, was subsequently fired in a seemingly very similar supermarket company where he had great difficulty operating in a leveraged environment where resources were very scarce.

Some organizations are simple, dealing with a homogenous product or suite of services. Some are extremely complex and require a completely different set of organizational skills. Does your new CEO or senior executive really need to have specific industry or product knowledge? Or is best practices a bigger concern? Just be careful that you fully understand what really drives your business. If excellent personal customer service is what really built your company, it would probably be a big mistake to bring in a new CEO with a GE model mindset.

EXAMPLE (CEO)

- Providing the leadership that sustains improvement in operations and service

- Formulating the organization's goals, priorities, and policies in conjunction with the Board of Commissioners;

- Planning and executing policies, programs, and projects;

- Making all leadership decisions that direct the daily operation;

- Regularly informing, recommending to, and communicating with the Board of Commissioners concerning operations, fiscal status, projects and opportunities;

- Ensuring the financial integrity and controlling the financial assets;

- Communicating effectively with local, state and federal officials; the news media, public and social service agencies; business organizations and representatives; neighborhood and community groups; resident councils; and employees and contractors;

- Negotiating effectively with business and government entities;

- Compose or review, and then approve the reports and documents required by federal, state and local jurisdictions;

- Advise the Residents Councils by attending regularly scheduled meetings to brief the representative officers on new or proposed changes in policies and procedures, maintenance problems and other areas that may affect residents; and

- Attend professional conferences, training sessions and seminars to explore new concepts, trends and activities in the field of housing management.

EXAMPLE (SVP)

- Responsible for total store operations, as well as merchandising, loss prevention, marketing, advertising, industrial engineering, customer service, store design and store maintenance.

- Interact with chief executive and chief financial officers as a part of a three person internal board of directors to establish corporate strategic and tactical plans

- Responsible for maintaining world class merchandising and marketing programs. This does not necessarily mean leading the industry, just selecting the best of what has been tried and proven.

- Responsible for improving store level employee morale and retention.

- Responsible for maintaining excellent store conditions and service levels while minimizing expenses

- Responsible for top-grading in all departments, at all levels

- Supervise vice presidents of marketing, merchandising, operations, loss prevention, store operations support, customer service and maintenance.

TEN

Leadership Attributes

Identify the key leadership capabilities necessary. Remember that leadership is about moving the troops toward a desired outcome. Leadership is about facilitating desired change. *Our experience has shown us time and again that for the most part, organizations are over-managed and under-led.* Extreme care should be employed here to establish just what kinds of leadership skills and attributes are necessary and desirable in a particular role. Do not forget to think about how the candidate's leadership requirements might change down the road.

Consider closely the environment in which the candidate will be expected to operate. Ideally, he or she should have proven ability to lead in similar situations, with similar autonomy, resources, support and competitive landscape, just to name a few. Also consider that different leaders thrive in different situations, including turn-around scenarios, rapid growth periods and maintenance mode.

The finest leaders treat everybody incredibly well and lead with a bit of humility. I have found that when I go into a company to lead, it is important to have a plan and to make that plan a simple one that everybody can understand. I am constantly asking the question, "What are the two or three levers that, if done right, if pulled correctly, will really turn this business? What are the two or three things that really matter?" And I find that most leaders do not really do that often. They just dive into all this detail and start doing stuff.

Is leading with humility important in your organization? I cannot imagine why it would not be but this is a question that needs to be asked and answered.

I am going to repeat what I stated earlier. High performance leaders lead consistently in a manner that inspires others to trust and follow them. They know how to connect with the workforce in such a manner that everyone in the organization understands the mission at hand. They are involved in all of the critical areas of the business: strategy, people systems and operations. They are not micromanagers by any means, but they are fully aware of what is going on in their business. They understand what drives the business.

High performance leaders encourage their leadership teams to stretch and achieve while holding everyone accountable for their performance, behavior and promises. High performance leaders, unlike managers help their organization cope with ambiguity by crystallizing the end objective, painting the vision, assigning priorities, separating the wheat from the chaff, and providing a laser like focus. High performance leaders do not know it all. They know what they do not know. They understand their own strengths, weaknesses and propensities; and they delegate and compensate accordingly. High performance leaders share information, resources and credit effectively. They understand that there is no limit to what can be accomplished if they do not care who gets the credit.

High performance leaders are real people. They are not afraid to show vulnerability, admit mistakes and ask for help. They are constantly communicating their company's vision, purpose and values. These high performance leaders are constantly mindful of customers, end users and their rank-in-file employees. High performance leaders are decisive yet not reckless. They understand that a good plan well executed beats an ironclad plan with mediocre execution every time. These people understand that all employees deep down want to do a good job and want to feel like they are making a contribution. They understand that we are all looking for leadership.

High performance leaders are confident yet not arrogant. They are in constant contact with their organization to the extent they can feel the pulse; their constituents feel a connection with them. High performance leaders have a sense of humor and the ability to make the job fun. They understand the power of a workforce that is happy to see them, not afraid of them. These individuals are high integrity players. They mean and do what they say; they have no hidden agendas. Most high performance leaders are story tellers. They teach by telling stories and using anecdotes and metaphors to illustrate their points and put things in perspective. These people instill passion in others and energize their workforces. They treat everyone with dignity and respect and they do not tolerate abuse of others.

ELEVEN

Specific Performance Expectations

One of the most important components of the needs analysis and certainly one of the most difficult; is establishing specific performance expectations for the incoming executive. This exercise is tricky because most of us are not accustomed to thinking through this process to this degree. What is helpful here is to "fast forward the tape" three months, six months, one year and two years past the date of the placement. How will you know that the new executive has been successful? How will the numbers look different? Will the organization look different? Will the capital structure be different?

Performance metrics should be specific, measurable and have a time table. They may or may not be tied directly to financial statements. This component is incredibly valuable on many levels. It gives the search a much sharper focus and moves far beyond the traditional job description that only focuses on background, experience and credentials. Make sure that when performance expectations are established, they are mindful of the company's financial condition, resource allocation model, competitive environment, labor relations situation and any other variable that could be a factor in impeding success in the position.

The needs analysis should clearly address the client's corporate or high level strategic issues. We are careful not to assume that the latest annual report, or the plaque hanging in the office, paints an accurate picture. The consultant must be clear about what drives the client's business, what differentiates the client from its competitors, where the client wants to take the business, as well as what strengths, weaknesses, opportunities and threats exist.

EXAMPLE (CEO)

- Conceptualize new go-to-market strategy for board review by first quarter 2011

- Reverse sales trends by 5 percentage points years 1 through 3 with +5 percent of baseline as objective for FY 2013

- Improve EBITDA by 500 basis points years 1 through 3

- Conceptualize market diversification strategy for board approval by second quarter 2011

- Design a new prototype format for rollout by the end of the fourth quarter

- Grow same store sales by 5 percent (running rate) by the end of the fourth quarter

- Reduce store level turnover by 2 percent per quarter by the end of the second quarter

EXAMPLE 2 (SVP)

- Develop an objective scoring system to quantify store standards by the end of first quarter with the objective of raising the overall company standard by 20 points by year's end

- Develop and implement an inventory loss program by the end of the first quarter with the objective of reducing non-perishable shrink from its current level of 1.8 percent to 1.0 percent by year's end

- Develop and implement a plan by the end of the first quarter to raise trade discounts and allowances from the current 3.5 percent of sales to 4.25 percent of sales by the fourth quarter

- Reduce cash and check loss from $1,785 PSPM to $1,000 PSPM (running rate) by the fourth quarter

- Engineer a total shopping experience blueprint, choreographing each stage of the customer's experience to have ready to present to board of directors by the end of the third quarter

- Design a new prototype store capable of housing our current 45,000 SKU's with the objective of reducing building and operating costs by 10 percent without sacrificing ambiance by the end of the fourth quarter

- Assemble and manage a task force to survey and tour top retailers world-wide in an exercise of determining the best mix of store merchandising fixtures for the new prototype store

- Grow same store sales by 5 percent (running rate) by the end of the fourth quarter

- Develop and implement a program to reduce store level turnover by 2 percent per quarter by the end of the second quarter

- Design and implement a customer satisfaction/ complaint tracking system with the objective of reducing customer complaints by 25 percent by the end of the fourth quarter

TWELVE

Cast a Wide Net

The second piece of our search roadmap, following the needs analysis, is the target list, which essentially tells us where we are going to look in order to assemble a pool of potential candidates.

Every search is different and requires a new strategy; therefore, it is important that we communicate with the client with respect to exactly where we are searching in an effort to locate the best possible candidates for a particular opportunity. In our case, we are also obligated to advise our clients of existing client relationships that might preclude Allen Austin from recruiting for particular companies.

Sometimes the ideal candidates will come from within the client's industry and from their direct competitors; and sometimes they will come from other industries in which best practices in a particular discipline are better. For example, if a supermarket retail company is looking for a vice president of real estate, the person with the best skill set for that job may not exist within that industry.

Indeed, in many cases, candidates from outside a particular industry can be as, or more effective, than players within the industry. These determinations are always made as a result of collaboration. While we make recommendations, and many times all or most of our recommendations are accepted, we require buy-in on all phases of each search.

Assuming that the client's needs analysis and target list is complete and that all involved have signed off on all documents, Allen

Austin's next objective is to cast the widest possible net to sell the opportunity, not the candidate; and to build a pool of as many potential candidates as we possibly can.

Building a large pool of candidates is important to Allen Austin because we do not want to limit our choices to just three to five great candidates; we want to go through the entire target list which has been agreed upon by both client and consultant and that list may often consist of 150-200 candidates or more. We must be certain that we have thoroughly examined the entire target list. Although there may, in some cases, be only a dozen candidates in the country, or the world, that could do a certain job effectively, that is not normally the case.

If you are not utilizing the services of a professional firm, you will still want to follow a similar process of sourcing and identifying a suitable number of candidates. The trickiest parts of securing an adequate candidate pool when you are recruiting directly in to your company is actually making enough direct contacts, while keeping the playing field level and remaining objective.

Unless you are doing a search to replace Jack Welch at General Electric, or some other search in which the candidate pool is necessarily miniscule, the general rule is that you had better start with a target list of at least 150 potential candidates. I repeat – AT LEAST 150 potential candidates. In most cases the numbers should be greater. There is no way to quote a number that would be appropriate for each situation. The numbers are search specific.

Philosophically, your initial target list should consist of virtually every possible candidate who would be a logical fit for your particular search. This axiom would apply to any CEO or officer level search in a traditional industry.

EXAMPLE 1

> We were retained to find a CEO to replace an incumbent chief executive. After a lengthy discussion with the client, it was determined that the individual we were looking for

would certainly have a senior level general management and deal-making background in commercial real estate.

We had identified 268 senior commercial real estate brokers in, and around, Houston.

We contacted all of the 268 individuals on our target list. We were referred to another twenty-five or so. We procured forty-seven fresh resumes, determined that thirty-one were qualified, interviewed twelve and presented three. Because we had cast a wide enough net, and interviewed based on not only the hard skills required, but also the personality traits needed, the search was successful. An ideal candidate was hired and the client's expectations were clearly exceeded.

EXAMPLE 2

We were retained to find a CEO for a Dallas-owned, Chicago-based vinyl composite tile manufacturing company. The company was in crisis. We needed a turnaround specialist, a wizard, a water-walker. After three days of discussions with the owner and interim CEO, a detailed search specification had been developed and approved by the owner and interim CEO. It was also determined that we needed to be talking to substantially every sitting Chicago based CEO and COO in a manufacturing environment with revenues between $20 million and $100 million. We needed to cast as wide a net as possible in order to surface not just a good candidate, but the absolute best possible candidate. Second best would not do. It was also decided that looking outside of Chicago should not be necessary given Chicago is the manufacturing capital of the world.

A Hoovers query revealed 534 companies in Greater Chicago that fit this description. We had our marching orders. We contacted substantially everyone on the original target list. We delivered a short (less than one minute), concise, hard-hitting presentation in each of our phone calls. We asked for referrals and advice. In other words, we did not leave a stone unturned. The 500+ individuals we talked to referred Allen Austin to approximately 100 additional candidates.

We procured eighty fresh resumes. Not resumes we found on the internet, or fished out of an old file or database, or pulled from some informal network. These were eighty new resumes on COOs that were not actively looking, were not reading ads, and not posting their resumes on the net. We could honestly say that our pool of resumes represented the cream of the crop, the best of the best, in Chicago.

A screening and interviewing process, which is not the subject of this discussion, took place, and we ultimately presented three motivated, qualified candidates, all of whom had led at least two turnarounds. The candidate was hired and subsequently has performed brilliantly. The search was text-book perfect.

EXAMPLE 3

We were retained to conduct a search for a Chief Merchandising Officer. The client was the brand new CEO of the 47th largest supermarket chain in the country.

Time was of the essence, so we assembled a target list of 268 target candidates, virtually every possible merchandising executive from the top retail and wholesale operations in the country. In two weeks we had contacted substantially all of our prospects, procured sixty-one resumes, determined thirty were qualified and had interviewed and qualified our list of twelve semi-finalists.

The length of time between the point at which the search was commissioned and the time of acceptance of our client's offer, was forty-four days.

I could cite hundreds more examples of extremely successful searches completed as a direct result of this methodology. The benefit of careful preparation and research cannot be overestimated.

THIRTEEN

Discovery and Interview Process

One important aspect in fine tuning is to "flush out the fisherman" i.e., those candidates who are just curious or just open to exploring other opportunities. There are plenty of candidates who are willing to go along for the ride just to see what an alternative offer might look like; or to parlay an offer from our client in to a counter-offer from their current employer.

Some people just have the attitude "Nothing ventured nothing gained", with little or no regard to what inconvenience, heartache or heartburn their fishing expedition might cause for us, our client and for that matter, other candidates who are sincerely interested in the position for the right reasons. Unfortunately, such candidates are increasingly common.

Be aware. Be VERY aware and AFRAID of the first impression! Most of the time we make bad hiring decisions because we decide too soon: we are too emotional, we do not know what we are looking for or we do not know what questions to ask. Remember that traditional techniques used by most managers are seriously flawed and produce results just marginally better than a flip of the coin. Even the most exhaustive processes come down to a decision based on gut feeling, instinct and intuition more often than not.

Many A Players are overlooked because they do not meet some superficial standard, or because they do not perform brilliantly during the interview. Most managers just do not realize that some of the most stellar performers are not great interviewers. Conversely, there are many "professional interviewees," who are substandard performers. Many of these candidates who perform so remarkably in interviews do so because they have so much experience! Trust me when I tell you that your candidate's superior interviewing skills will not add one iota of value to your company once he or she is hired.

In David Adler's Snap Decisions, he says that cognitive psychologists and decision theorists believe we have two decision systems at our disposal: (1) those that come from the gut, and (2) those that originate in the mind.

Gut decisions are very quick, based on intuition or first impressions. These are snap judgments that occur almost instantaneously, in the blink of an eye, with little deliberation. This decision system works well in certain areas of life.

He goes on to say that this system does not work well in many modern situations such as investing, hiring, and other complex scenarios. To make more complex decisions, we humans need to rely on the second type of decision system, which takes much longer and involves analysis.

Our intuitive system is not designed to handle abstract problems, which is why we have so much trouble selecting a 401(k) investment, knowing when to sell a stock, compounding interest rates, or dealing with probabilities and statistics in general. It's why many people believed real estate could only go up, or after the crash, that it could only go down. It's why investment bank CEOs, based on their decade-long success, began to think they could do no wrong. It's why a manager hires the wrong employee who seemed so charming at the job interview. And it's why economic "experts" underestimated the risks of credit markets and did not see the growing possibility of a systemic meltdown.

Another problem is that most managers assume that effective recruiting is a selling proposition. Many A Players are driven away by managers who oversell the position, therefore cheapening it. Successful recruiting is more of a buying situation, rather than a selling situation. Candidates should be required to earn the right to a valuable job; and then to sell you.

In order to further qualify potential candidates against our client's expectations and values, we will ask those candidates who have agreed to go through the process to spend an average of eight to ten hours in filling out very detailed, essay-type questionnaires. This discovery process will ultimately reveal, in large part, which candidates are best suited for our client's situation. We call this process the 4C assessment.

Allen Austin's 4C assessment focuses on candidate self-evaluation: contribution, culture, character and commitment. It also gives my firm a very good sense of the candidate's writing, thinking, and reasoning styles. Additionally, we gain some insight into how well they follow instructions and can articulate answers to complex questions; and it gives us a good sense of how cooperative or arrogant they might be on the job. Based on our experience, a candidate who is uncooperative and unresponsive to our requests during the screening process will more than likely perform in the same manner once they are working for the client's company. Indeed, the candidate's personality is often just as important as their background, experience, credentials and skill sets.

This process is unique and it is something we have determined we cannot do without, as it has saved Allen Austin from following through with candidates who more than likely would have ultimately failed. The 4C assessment is essentially a self-appraisal for the candidate, as it forces them to answer questions about themselves that may have never occurred to them just as our needs analysis performs a similar function for our clients. Many of our candidates have told us they learned more about themselves while going through this process than they had at any other point in their career.

The questionnaire typically helps a candidate to understand, at a much deeper level, what would be required of them in order to be successful in our client's position. In some cases, they come to realize that the job is not a good match for their talents or needs. In such instances, the candidate may, with good reason, self-select out of a process that they would have otherwise continued.

This discovery process typically eliminates the marginally qualified as well as the casually interested; we are usually left with a dozen or so candidates with whom we are really impressed, and who have provided answers with which we are comfortable. In some cases our clients have wanted to be involved in the screening process and have read the semi-finalists' responses. In those cases we have agreed on finalists with whom we want to move forward.

It is worth mentioning here that 98 percent of candidates who endure this process accept employment offers extended by our clients. A recent study of 44 Fortune 500 companies that did at least thirty retained searches per year revealed that 29 percent of offers extended through search firms in the study were rejected. It should not surprise anyone that roughly 45 percent of those placed as a result of this lack of process will wash out within eighteen months.

We then typically conduct face-to-face interviews with our semi-finalist pool of select candidates. During which, we assess such qualities as personal presence and the ability to persuade qualities which are crucial in a candidate for any senior level position.

If you are not using a search firm, you will dramatically improve your odds if you will require all prospective candidates to go through a series of exercises.

EXAMPLE

I.   SELF-APPRAISAL

    a. Describe the best job you have ever had and specifically what made it so.

    b. Give me a thorough self-appraisal, beginning with what you consider your strengths & assets.

    c. Please describe your weaknesses and areas for improvement along with what kinds of things you have done to compensate for your shortcomings.

d. Give me a comprehensive wish list of ALL attributes you would like to have in your next role.

e. Give me a comprehensive list of ALL attributes you want to avoid in your next role.

II.   LEADERSHIP/ATTRIBUTES

a. Tell me specifically about your successes in leading consistently in a way that inspires others to follow and trust you.

b. How would your subordinates describe your energy and bias for action and your ability to ensure quality execution?

c. Tell me about how you stay intimately involved in your organization's strategy, people systems and operations.

d. How would you describe your propensity to hold people in your organization accountable for their performance, behavior, and promises?

e. Please describe how you help a complex organization deal with ambiguity and multiple priorities.

f. What would your stakeholders feel are your strengths and shortcomings in terms of delegating critical and important tasks to others?

g. What would your stakeholders feel are your strengths and shortcomings in terms of sharing information, resources and credit?

h. Describe a situation in which you had to admit and demonstrate that you were a real person, not afraid to show vulnerability, admit mistakes and ask for help.

i. How would your past stakeholders describe your approach to communicating your company's vision, purpose and values?

j. Talk to me about how your communication of your organization's values is manifested in your rank and file employees.

k. Describe a situation in which you had to utilize inductive reasoning to gather a broad range of data from your environment, draw conclusions, explain and add calm and clarity to the situation, separating emotion from logic.

l. Describe a situation in which you had to tell a stakeholder the truth even when it was not what he or she wanted to hear.

m. Describe a situation in which you demonstrated that you were in the fight for the long haul, not just for the short run or good times.

n. Describe a situation in which your sense of humor, lightheartedness and/or willingness to laugh at yourself defused a tense situation.

o. Describe a situation in which you helped a stakeholder put their issues in context by use of anecdotes, metaphors and war stories.

p. Describe your approach to instilling passion and energizing your workforce.

q. Describe how you lead by example in encouraging your management team to treat others with dignity and respect.

III. **MANAGEMENT**

a. How would you describe your relationship management experience, philosophy and style?

b. Please describe your experience in strategic planning and implementation, including successful and unsuccessful approaches.

c. What would your subordinates feel are your strengths and shortcomings in terms of consensus building and conflict management?

d. How would past superiors describe your approaches to profitable project management and follow through?

e. Describe the process you utilized to track and achieve benchmark metrics against known best practices? Describe a situation in which you had to effectively track, monitor and document complex processes.

f. Describe a complex situation in which you had to analyze the situation and solve a problem quickly.

g. Please describe a situation in which you had to prepare and deliver an impactful presentation to a group of executive decision makers.

h. Do you consider yourself a better Mr. Inside or Mr. Outside, and why?

i. Are you more likely to find yourself asking for forgiveness or permission?

j. What is your perspective on sales & marketing's involvement with the client support process? What arrangement do you feel works best?

IV. INTERPERSONAL COMPETENCIES

a. Describe situations in which your commitment to integrity caused you discomfort.

b. Give examples of your going beyond what was normally expected to enhance your company's reputation or image.

c. Describe a situation in which your stamina was tested.

d. How did you grow so passionate about your profession?

e. Discuss your methods of diagnosing and exceeding client/customer needs.

f. Are you familiar with the term "active listening"? How would you definite it?

g. How do you motivate co-workers outside your team?

h. How would you rate yourself in terms of compassion, transparency and vulnerability? Why?

V. **FIT/ALIGNMENT/TRANSITION**

a. Capsulate your knowledge of your industry and what makes it tick.

a. Other than what you have learned from Allen Austin and read in our literature, what do you know about the opportunity you have been presented?

b. Why do you believe this is the right fit for you at this point in your career?

c. What would it take for you to make a career change? Why move now?

d. What actions would you take in the first weeks?

e. How many meaningful contacts might you have within your chosen field of focus?

f. Having spoken with me, and having read the position description, what challenges do you see?

g. What would your exit strategy be to leave your current employment?

h. When could you be available to begin?

FOURTEEN

Evaluating the Candidate

Regardless of the nature or scope of the position they hold, successful people do certain things that unsuccessful people do not. Successful people are successful time and time again, over long periods of time. Success is never a surprise or an isolated event.

Unsuccessful people seem to always miss the mark in one area or another, whether it is people skills, organizational ability, commitment or technical competence. Measuring past performance is the best predictor of future success. Great managers also have a consistent track record of hiring great people.

Weak interviewers seem to fall into three broad categories. The first category includes those who are too emotional. These are the ones who make very quick decisions based on first impressions and personality. The second category includes those who are overly intuitive, to the extent that they short-circuit the process, superficially assessing only a narrow group of attributes. Finally, the technical interviewer is great at fact-finding, but lacks decisiveness.

Effective hiring constitutes 80 percent of a manager's success. If we are to deliver A Players and great managers to our client-companies and firms, we must assure ourselves we are presenting candidates with a record of hiring great people. One of the ways to get to the root of this challenge is to ask your candidate to describe his or her hiring successes and failures. Because the selection process is tedious and time consuming, most of us have a tendency to fall prey to the energetic, attractive, affable and articulate candidate who many times will fall far short of expectations once on the job.

The very best interviewers and hiring managers understand that the hiring decision must be intuitive to some extent. There is never enough information to match abilities, needs, and interests completely. Despite the intuitive component, they recognize that the hiring decision must be based on an analytical, fact-finding process. Therefore, if the client's job description requires someone who can operate in a highly leveraged or a resource-strained environment, we will probably look for a candidate who has performed successfully in a leveraged environment in the past. We have seen plenty of CEOs who could do a fabulous job in a situation where the company is relatively debt-free and has ample resources, but they could not function well when they were put in an environment where they were resource-constrained, the company was highly leveraged, and 90 percent of their EBIDTA had to go to service debt.

One great idea we have seen used many times is to ask your potential executive to write a document detailing a charter of his or her past organization, or to articulate his or her vision for your organization in charter format.

EXAMPLE

Our organization operates with total integrity. This is to say that there are no gray issues in terms of honesty or integrity. We are not here to kid each other or to make the numbers or conditions appear other than they really are. We call a spade a spade. We communicate with total honesty. Honesty is appreciated and expected. Messengers are not shot. Surprises are not received well. The charlatan is shot.

Integrity means being totally honest with superiors. It means telling the truth, whether it feels right or not. The senior leadership of the company deserves to know the truth. They are responsible for finding out the truth. Putting on a show serves no useful purpose.

It also means being totally honest with subordinates. Everyone in our organization deserves to know exactly where they stand in terms of promotional possibilities, disciplinary issues and even possible termination. For example, an associate that is being terminated or promoted should never be surprised.

Integrity also means acting in the best interest of the company. It means not playing games to minimize "shrink" at the expense of gross margin by buying in on items that carry no cost advantage, only "shrink gain." To go a step further, integrity means making sure that all reporting systems are reporting the actual, not a "doctored figure."

In summary, integrity means being totally honest in everything you do and expecting the same of your organization. There is no such thing as minor theft. There is no such thing as minor fabrication of the truth. Integrity is the cornerstone of everything we do.

CONTINUOUS IMPROVEMENT

We believe strongly in the concept of continuous improvement. In short, this means that while we certainly will celebrate the superior performance of the day, we will never be totally satisfied with our performance. We will always be hungry for improvement. We are always looking for productivity enhancements, potential cost savings, sales enhancements, margin dollar improvements, overhead reductions, store standards improvements, associate quality improvement, and personal improvement. We realize that no individual, no organization, ever stands still; we are either improving or declining, and we are determined to improve constantly. We solicit feedback from the total organization in order to utilize and recognize the total organization in this process. We celebrate and recognize even the smallest contribution to improvement. Continuous improvement is a common thread that runs through all of our endeavors toward achieving legendary service leadership.

The leaders in our organization are passionate about the business. We are students of the business. We want to know everything we can about the business and we put systems in place to ensure that our organization learns maximum amounts of information from competitors, trade journals and business publications.

We are committed to improving our operation each and every time we enter a store.

FINANCIAL

Our overall objective as it relates to "the numbers" is to optimize financial performance for the store, the district, the region and the company in keeping with our philosophy of continuous improvement.

In addition, we take ownership for the sales and gross profit lines, as a sole proprietor would. We realize that over the long term, the operations team has more impact on sales than any other. This is not to downplay the importance of the marketing effort, for we play a very important role in that regard. We realize that through legendary service leadership and superior store operations, that we have more long term impact on sales and profits than any other discipline.

We pay attention to all factors in the market. We are acutely aware of all of the competitive activity within our markets. We are aware of the economic environment as well. In short, we are totally aware of our external environment and are able to discuss externalities intelligently with all. We provide feedback and recommendations to those who can assist us in dealing with our external environment; we may even be very persistent along these lines. We do not, however, dwell on things that we do not control. After having made our recommendations to senior management at the service center with regard to marketing and administrative issues, we concentrate on the issues that we control entirely.

PEOPLE

We realize that people are our most important asset. As a result, we spend a major portion of our time developing our organizations.

We know who our strongest players are in every role and we are intimately familiar with management personnel at least two levels deep in the organization. We concentrate on our strong players in that we insure that they are continuing to move ahead both personally and professionally. We keep them challenged, provide them autonomy, and use them as organizational resources. We realize the value of these informal leaders; we recognize and allow them to lead in ways that benefit the individual and the organization.

We also know where our weaknesses are. Many of our weak players are new. Others have lost the vision, or have somehow become distracted or disillusioned. We realize that a chain is only as strong as its weakest link and that it is our responsibility to improve or replace individuals who for one reason or another contaminate the winner's circle. Our weak players who are in trouble are given every chance to succeed, but they know exactly where they stand. When the unfortunate does occur, when we do have to terminate or demote, it is never a surprise to the subject. They have been given more than a fair opportunity to correct any deficiency that might exist. We face conflict and poor performance head on and take decisive action when and where it is called for.

We do not abuse, or tolerate the abuse of people in any case. While we recognize the value of discipline, we are situational leaders who praise in public and conduct constructive criticism in private. We are always careful not to demoralize. We always maintain or enhance self esteem when criticizing.

We use meetings for information, recognition and decision making, that's all! We <u>never</u> use the meeting format for criticism because we recognize that this activity is best done one-on-one, in private.

We are also aware that, because we require much of our associates, it is critically important that we have fun at work. We believe in this so much that we actually plan fun, and we plan it often! We have associate dress-up days, appreciation days, associate and family outings and an array of other activities to show our people that we appreciate their efforts.

We make every effort to keep our organization stable. We move people only when it makes perfect sense. When we do make moves, the person(s) involved know where they are going, why they are going there, what their role will be, how their strengths will complement their new peers and how their new environment will compliment or augment their strengths.

STORES

We are keenly aware of our objective as it relates to store conditions. Our objective is to have store conditions and a total shopping experience that is noticeably better than the competition. We pay much attention to detail and subscribe to the philosophy that everything has a place and every place has a thing. We realize that superior store standards have a positive impact on associate morale and pride, as well as customer perception. We are absolutely determined to have sparkling clean, well merchandised, well-organized sales floors, back rooms, break rooms and restrooms at all times.

CUSTOMERS

We strive to provide legendary service every day, on every shift. We accomplish this level of service by constantly observing our personnel in action and by setting the right example. We are all members of the quarter fine club. We are absolutely committed to our "Pledge to Keep Our Customers Coming Back" and we insist on compliance to the "eight points." We make it a point, at every level, to recognize associates individually (catch them doing it right) for specific acts of good service, and we also make it a point to correct associates who have "not gotten it right" yet. We realize that legendary service is the key to our competitive future and we give it our all every day.

We realize that Legendary Service is an attitude, a mindset; it is not added hours or resources. Adding resources does not result in legendary service. The right commitment does.

MERCHANDISING

We realize that our primary mission along these lines is to build the business. We are merchants, not just shrink controllers. This is not to say that we are not concerned about shrink; we utilize all of the tools at our disposal to control shrink. We date our coolers and strictly enforce the 3X program in our meat coolers. We carefully analyze our movement records when writing orders. In addition, we pay close attention to sanitation and rotation. Still, we are merchants. We have systems in place to ensure that we fully support all ads and have total variety. We realize that perishables, in terms of product merchandising, are our primary vehicle to differentiate ourselves from the competition.

We strive to build our FRESH image. FRESH is a critical component as it relates to produce, meat, seafood, floral, cheese shops, salad bars, deli and bakery. We adhere strictly to our dating standards and pay close attention to the appearance of all of our perishable case merchandising and products. We never leave merchandise in our counters or cases that we would not be proud to take home.

We make sure that all of our cases are sparkling clean. We take the responsibility for scheduling the cleaning of all of our perishable cases on a regular basis.

TEAMWORK

We operate under the philosophy that Top's is a team. None of us is as smart as all of us. We are not dependent or independent. We are interdependent. This is to say that the total organization comes first. An example - The Marine Corps has a code.....Unit - Corps - God - Country. Our code is Company - Region - District - Store - Individual. Our code does not diminish the importance of the individual, for the company is composed of individuals, all of who are important. Our code does imply that all decisions must be made with the good of the total company, region, district, store and individual in mind. Each individual has a responsibility to make a meaningful contribution to their unit.

It is our responsibility to contribute to the overall success of the company. It is the responsibility of our associates at the service center to serve us. It is our responsibility to become easy to serve.

We are competitive by nature. We enjoy comparing numbers with our peers, but our focus is on beating the competition -- the other supermarkets in our trade areas.

It is our responsibility to serve with total dedication. We operate in a safe environment that encourages each core associate to speak their mind, the right way. This is to say that we have a responsibility to fight for what we believe in, for what we stand for. We understand however that it is easy to criticize, condemn and complain. When we disagree with a particular course of action or philosophy, we express our concerns diplomatically and respectfully, and we are prepared to offer suggestions that we truly believe are better alternatives.

We understand that there will be times when we must execute a course of action that we would not have chosen. At the instant it becomes clear the orders are firm, it is our responsibility to execute flawlessly and with conviction. We take ownership and responsibility for the particular mission at hand. We assume the corporate, regional, district, or store position and are prepared to defend and explain the action. We understand our responsibility is to support, communicate and execute the mission of the company, region, district, and store.

In summary, we constantly strive for continuous improvement. We are proud of the accomplishments of the past and we experience ambitious dissatisfaction in every area of our operation.

This is just one example you could consider. My point here is that you are taking an enormous risk when you bring an outside CEO or executive in to your business. The cost of a mis-hire is enormous. Spend enough time evaluating your candidate to get really comfortable that he or she can succeed in your environment. Remember that roughly 45 percent of all newly placed senior executives will quit, be fired or otherwise forced out in scenarios in which standard hiring practices are used.

Be aware of the Superstar. In 2007, I attended Harvard Business School's program entitled *Leading Professional Service Firms*. I learned a great deal about the way global professional services firms work. I also learned that it is very common for these kinds of firms (and for that matter, all companies) to want to hire the competition's superstars. While the best predictor of future performance is in fact past performance, this is a very slippery slope. What must be considered if you are to hire the superstar from your competition are all of the variables responsible for your potential future superstar's success. We often make the mistake of looking at performance in a vacuum.

Throughout this book, we've been examining all of the variables associated with a successful placement of a CEO or senior executive. Stack the odds in your favor and consider all of the critical success factors we have been talking about.

FIFTEEN

Checking References

Before presenting any of our final candidates to the client, we perform one of our key tasks a 58 point Reference Audit involving a 360-degree reference check process with two superiors, two subordinates and two peers of *our* choosing. Most reference checks are worthless, or nearly so in our opinion, because they are done in advance of an offer to a candidate that the client has already met with; and they are done at a point in the process where everyone involved, including key figures at the client company and the search consultant perhaps a dozen people, in some cases are already emotionally committed to the candidate. At that point any reference check that takes place is merely an afterthought/formality; a dot the "I" or cross the "T" type of exercise that does not really have any discovery value. In the worst case scenario, the person who is conducting the reference check is essentially leading the witness.

We approach reference checking from a different angle. We typically start the search process by telling the candidate, in effect, "We understand you are interested in this position, and we are happy and excited to be working with you, but we will only allow you to go through this process if it looks like it is going to be a good deal for you, as well as for our client. Therefore, it is important that you be honest, candid and forthright with us through the entire process." We always tell the candidate upfront that towards the end of the process we will verify whatever they tell us with respect to such typical references as dates of employment, compensation and whether or not they are eligible for rehire. It is certainly possible to check references on people who are actively employed; you have to be discreet, but in most cases it is very doable.

When interviewing references we emphasize that it is very important that we have 25 - 30 minutes of quality time to discuss the candidate and his or her propensities, attributes and proclivities. We want to make sure that whatever a candidate brings to the table is very closely aligned with our client's expectations, values and mission, the way they do business, the way they allocate resources and the way they manage and lead. We will ask the reference to rate the candidate objectively with respect to 58 key attributes that we have identified, along with our client, as being necessary for the candidate's success in that particular position. Essentially, we ask each reference to do much the same thing that we do whenever we start a search; and that is to not even think about the particular position we are discussing, but to simply talk to us openly about the candidate what types of environments in which they would flourish, as well as what types of environments they would feel constrained or held back.

During this process we feel that it is essential to talk to a representative sample of the candidates' peers, people they have worked across the table with; subordinates people who have worked for them and know what their hot buttons are; and their superiors the people who have assigned them tasks. In doing so we strive to obtain a very clear, 360-degree picture of the way this candidate operates, because candidates are just like client-companies in many cases, they do not understand themselves nearly as well as the people who have observed them at work.

We are always careful to tell everyone involved in the reference checking process that *we are not trying to summarily dismiss people; we are simply trying to uncover all of the variables that could conceivably cause a search or a placement to go awry.* It is a very detailed process, and it takes a lot of listening and insight to really understand the results. In some instances, references have told us that they did not think a candidate or their family would be happy living in the area where the client company is located, That is just one of many amazingly revealing insights we gain by spending four to six hours doing these kinds of reference checks on each candidate.

We will then do a full write-up on all of these reference checks; we will identify who we have talked to, but we do not specifically identify who said what (the reference) and we make that clear to the references we interview so they can be comfortable in talking with us. In many cases we will meet with the client to discuss any potential concerns that have come to light during the process. We believe that if there are potential issues i.e., the candidate's family is reluctant to move, or the candidate has previously been unhappy with the autocratic management style of a particular board or CEO then the client needs to know about those things sooner rather than later.

Obtaining this kind of candid feedback from references when you are the direct employer will be very challenging.

Reference checking text book perfection in my view is the scenario in which:

- You, the hiring manager (usually a board member or CEO) are highly skilled at interviewing, active listening and have the time to personally check references of all of your impact players

- The reference with whom you are speaking feels very comfortable giving you honest, open and candid feedback on all matters involving your potential candidate's fit quotient.

- The challenge here is that this scenario almost never exists. Rarely will a C-level executive or board member take the time or have the inclination to personally check references. Additionally, the instances in which references are going to be willing to be totally honest with you or any of your staff, as a direct employer are extremely rare.

Second best to text book perfection and the best possible realistic solution is to insist that a Partner level search consultant conduct these very thorough and comprehensive reference audits. Never rely on the judgment of a junior level consultant, researcher or administrator. There is far too much at stake here.

Extremely talented human resource professionals are certainly capable of checking references in the manner I have recommended. The reference's willingness to be forthright and transparent will still almost always be an issue.

In the vast majority of cases, I recommend you outsource the reference checking to a professional you trust. Do not skimp here. It is just too important.

EXAMPLE

ATTRIBUTES	Number of References	Ref 1	Ref 2	Ref 3	Ref 4	Ref 5	Ref 6	Total	Reference Average	Candidate Self Rating
Thinking Skills										
Intelligence	6	9.0	10	10	9.0	10	9.0	57.0	9.50	8.00
Judgment	6	10	9.0	10	10	9.0	9.0	57.0	9.50	8.00
Decision Making	6	9.0	9.0	8.0	10	9.0	9.0	54.0	9.00	8.00
Creativity	6	8.0	7.0	8.0	6.0	8.0	8.0	45.0	7.50	6.00
Strategic skill	6	8.0	9.0	9.0	9.0	8.0	9.0	52.0	8.67	9.00
Pragmatism	6	9.0	9.0	9.0	9.0	10	8.0	54.0	9.00	10.0
Risk taking	6	8.0	7.0	6.0	8.0	7.0	5.0	41.0	6.83	5.00
Leading-edge perspective	6	7.0	7.0	8.0	5.0	6.0	8.0	41.0	6.83	5.00
Communications										
One-one	6	10	10	10	9.0	10	9.0	58.0	9.67	9.00
In meetings	6	9.0	9.0	8.0	10	9.0	9.0	54.0	9.00	9.00
Speeches	6	9.0	10	9.0	9.0	8.0	10	55.0	9.17	9.00
Written	6	8.0	6.0	7.0	8.0	6.0	7.0	42.0	7.00	9.00
Initiative										
Perseverance	6	10	9.0	9.0	10	9.0	10.	57.0	9.50	10.0
Independence	6	8.0	8.0	9.0	7.0	8.0	9.0	49.0	8.17	9.00
High standards	6	10	9.0	9.0	10	9.0	10	57.0	9.50	8.00
Adaptable	6	7.0	6.0	8.0	7.0	9.0	8.0	45.0	7.50	7.00
Stress Management										
Stress Mngmnt (general)	6	10	9.0	9.0	10	9.0	10.	57.0	9.50	8.00
Integrity	6	10	10	10	10	10	10	60.0	10.0	10.0
Self-awareness	6	8.0	9.0	9.0	8.0	9.0	10	53.0	8.83	8.00
Willingness to admit mistakes	6	9.0	10	9.0	10	9.0	9.0	56.0	9.33	7.00

Work Habits										
Time management	6	8.0	9.0	8.0	7.0	9.0	6.0	47.0	7.83	8.00
Organization/ planning	6	8.0	9.0	8.0	9.0	10	9.0	53.0	8.83	8.00
People Skills										
First impression made	6	9.0	10	9.0	10	10	9.0	57.0	9.50	7.00
Ability to win the liking and respect of people	6	9.0	9.0	8.0	6.0	9.0	9.0	50.0	8.33	7.00
Listening	6	9.0	9.0	10	9.0	8.0	10	55.0	9.17	7.00
Assertiveness	6	8.0	8.0	8.0	9.0	8.0	9.0	50.0	8.33	8.00
Political savvy	6	7.0	5.0	6.0	5.0	6.0	5.0	34.0	5.67	7.00
Willingness to take direction	6	8.0	8.0	7.0	8.0	6.0	7.0	44.0	7.33	8.00
Negotiating skills	6	9.0	9.0	10	9.0	9.0	10	56.0	9.33	9.00
Persuasion skills	6	10	10	9.0	10	9.0	9.0	57.0	9.50	9.00
Motivation										
Drive	6	9.0	9.0	10	9.0	9.0	8.0	54.0	9.00	9.00
Ambition	6	8.0	7.0	6.0	8.0	6.0	7.0	42.0	7.00	9.00
Customer focus	6	7.0	6.0	8.0	6.0	5.0	8.0	40.0	6.67	7.00
Enthusiasm	6	9.0	10	8.0	9.0	9.0	10	55.0	9.17	7.00
Tenacity	6	9.0	10	8.0	9.0	10	9.0	55.0	9.17	10.0
Balance in life	6	9.0	9.0	8.0	9.0	10	9.0	54.0	9.00	7.00
Leadership/ Management										
Leadership	6	9.0	9.0	10	9.0	9.0	9.0	55.0	9.17	7.00
Ability to hire the best people	6	9.0	10	9.0	10	9.0	9.0	56.0	9.33	9.00
Ability to train and coach	6	8.0	7.0	8.0	8.0	7.0	8.0	46.0	7.67	8.00
Willingness to remove the incompetent	6	6.0	5.0	5.0	6.0	4.0	6.0	32.0	5.33	8.00
Goal setting	6	8.0	9.0	9.0	10	10	9.0	55.0	9.17	9.00
Change management	6	10	9.0	9.0	9.0	8.0	9.0	54.0	9.00	9.00
Empowerment	6	10	9.0	9.0	10	9.0	9.0	56.0	9.33	9.00
Promoting diversity	3	NA	NA	10	9.0	NA	9.0	28.0	9.33	8.00
Monitoring performance	6	7.0	6.0	5.0	7.0	8.0	7.0	40.0	6.67	8.00
Building team efforts	6	9.0	9.0	10	10	9.0	10	57.0	9.50	8.00

SIXTEEN

Managing Expectations and Sealing the Deal

Allen Austin believes that continuity is important in any search. Because we have resisted the temptation to build layers of consultants in our practice, our partners are the ones to communicate directly with candidates who ultimately make the final cut, even in the earliest stages. As a result, our partners have a real relationship with each finalist candidate when it comes time to "seal the deal."

Sealing the deal in this sense has nothing whatsoever to do with coercion of any kind. Rather, it has to do with having developed a relationship with each candidate and having acquired specific knowledge about what constitutes a good move on the part of the candidate and his or her family. By the conclusion of each search, we have accumulated a rather lengthy list of reasons why this move is ideal for both candidate and client. This kind of philosophy usually results in a win-win situation for our clients and candidates; or as we say, a win-win-win. We like to win, too!

During this period when we are developing a relationship and a list of "reasons why," we are also assessing the candidate's expectations with regard to compensation, title, benefits, moving packages, contracts and the like. *Executed properly, there should be no surprises at the end of the search.* If expectations have been managed properly from the outset, our consultant should have a crystal clear picture of what our client is willing to offer and what our candidate is reasonably willing to accept. The operative term here is reasonably. If the move in question is all about compensation, it is not a good match.

We are consultants with a specialization in executive search. Our clients and our candidates depend on us to negotiate and mediate in such a manner that we create win-win scenarios. Here are some of our thoughts you may apply to your search. Most of this is coming from our perspective, but the principles still apply.

Negotiation of compensation must start in the early phases of the search. This process takes skill, intuition and probing. This process must start with a clear understanding of each candidate's motivation to make a move. Recall from the chapter on opportunity positioning that, in the ideal scenario, you are selling the opportunity and not the candidate.

We recommend concluding recruiting calls with an open-ended question such as "Are you aware of anyone I could or should be speaking with?" We ask the question in this manner in hopes that appropriate candidates will volunteer themselves as perfect candidates. Once we have established interest on the part of a particular candidate, we are then in perfect position to begin to ask, rather than answer, important questions. Once interest has been established, we respond by asking why the candidate him/herself may be interested.

This is the time to start listening actively and carefully. If you are to be successful in negotiating the compensation piece of the puzzle, you had better understand the candidate's motivation to move from the outset. After having asked the pivotal question, regarding the candidate's willingness to entertain the move, we could either qualify or disqualify the candidate based on his or her responses. Let us face it. Most candidates we approach would be willing to make a move for an unbelievable increase in compensation. The fact of the matter is that the average increase to make a lateral move, in terms of responsibility, even cases in which relocation is required, is 10 percent - 15 percent. There are many legitimate reasons to change employers. An increase in cash compensation, in and of itself, is rarely a legitimate reason.

If someone is to become and remain a legitimate candidate, they must demonstrate to you the willingness to make the move, and willingness to actively and enthusiastically pursue the job in question. Legitimate, primary reasons include:

- Lack of career opportunity with current employer, resultant of current employer's size, resources, geographic location or reach, reputation, quality of management, etc

- Enhanced career opportunity in terms of responsibility, visibility, personal growth or ability to work with a superior team of executives

- A dislike of a new direction or board of current employer

- A desire to join our client, who is larger, smaller, more progressive, more prestigious, more visible, more quality focused, more flexible, etc

- A strong desire to be in a more pleasing area of the county, such as the case in which a candidate wants to move to his or her home town or state, or to move closer to family

- A desire to participate in an equity sharing opportunity

An increase in cash compensation should be a secondary reason for making a change. When we conduct a search, we must establish in the very early stages of our search, the candidate's expectations in terms of cash compensation. Most of our clients, while having a compensation range in mind, want us to surface the best available talent based on our specification and let compensation be driven by the market. Regardless of your flexibility on compensation, it is important that you understand the candidate's expectations and the reasons for them.

This is one of the most complex processes relative to our task of managing expectations. There are cost-of-living issues, market issues, risk factors, reputation factors, and geographic factors, just to name a few. It could be that our client's locale has a cost-of-living substantially higher or lower. It could also be that the nature of the candidate's expertise puts him or her in a legitimate position to command a premium.

Our client could be in start-up or turn-around phase, or in danger of financial challenge; these are cases in which the candidate puts himself or herself at a higher risk relative to remaining with their current employer. In these cases, absent an equity opportunity, a premium cash compensation package possibly inclusive of large contingent bonuses or a lucrative commission schedule could be in order.

The list of variables is endless. The key here is to understand the candidate's rationale for his or her expectations. You must also be able to rationalize the legitimacy of your candidate's expectations in your own mind.

Here is an example of how we get down to the 'brass tacks' if you will. At the end of the process, we must nail down the candidate's bottom line. Possible questions include:

- John, assuming this opportunity is presented as we have discussed, what, in terms of cash compensation and incentives, would it take for you to accept an offer from my client?

- John, we both know there needs to be a cultural match between us. Assuming the fit is right, what are you going to require in terms of compensation to make this move?

- John, you and I both know that there are questions left to be answered; assuming your questions are answered satisfactorily, what kind of compensation and relocation package will you require?

- John, we are moving toward ultimate closure. You are, unless you tell me otherwise, going to be a finalist. Let us talk about compensation. What are your expectations?

- John, we are both realistic in terms of the risks and opportunities relative to this situation. Have you thought in specific terms what kind of compensation package my client would need to offer in order to procure your services?

The list of questions could go on. Be sure you are prepared with a strategy to address candidate expectations. Lack of skill in this area kills deals.

We are in the ultimate business of negotiating deals that make good business sense for both client and candidate. In addition, it is our job to ensure that, to the greatest extent possible; no offer is ever extended and then subsequently rejected.

Simply stated, we try to set the stage in such a manner that failure is virtually impossible. The textbook perfect scenario is one in which our client is pleased to offer more than the candidate expects; and one in which the candidate is prepared to accept less than our client is willing to offer.

Having set the stage perfectly, we have a very clear notion of both. We know the absolute number our candidate is prepared to accept. We know the parameters on which our client has based his or her expected offer.

In the perfect scenario, you will know the absolute bottom line cash compensation your candidate will accept. In addition, you will have given us latitude to negotiate within a certain range. Your picture-perfect client might have told you they would really like to hire your candidate at $165,000. You would ultimately like your client to say "I would very much like to hire Joe at $165,000. I am also willing to go to $185,000 if necessary. Act in our mutual best interest."

In this case, as in every case, our objective is to deliver an offer that marginally exceeds you candidate's expectations, while staying below you client's top-end offer. In other words, your objective is to deliver the ultimate win-win negotiation.

Let us examine a scenario in which your candidate has revised his expectations. Let us assume there is a substantial cost of living differential to the detriment of your candidate. Let us also assume that you have asked the final pivotal compensation question, to which your candidate's answer is, "I have thought long and hard about the offer and the cost of living in Chicago; I really am going to need $190,000 in order to make the move." You have two reasonable alternatives at this point. The first involves a take away strategy.

You might say, "John, I want to make sure I understand you; are you saying if this offer comes in at $185,000 you are going to turn it down? If he says he definitely would decline, your response should be: Are you also saying that if I could get you $190,000, you would definitively accept? In the event he says "yes," be sure to flush out any remaining issues at this point. Say to John, "I am not at all sure I can get the 190. We'll try. John, are there any other issues we need to discuss, or is this the only dangling issue?" If he responds in the affirmative, you say "John, if I can get the $190,000, when will you start?" We NEVER go back to our client with a counteroffer if there are unresolved issues, or without a start date.

In the absence of a search professional, you or someone in your organization will have to manage the expectations of your potential new executive.

SEVENTEEN

New Executive Integration

Once a candidate is hired, we conduct a formal follow-up process for a period of two years. We will typically check on the candidate's performance at intervals of one week; 30 days; 90 days; 180 days; one year; 18 months; and two years. In some cases, however, I have stayed in close contact with candidates on an informal basis for as long as 20 years.

During the follow-up stage, we try as best we can to assist both candidate and client with the executive integration and assimilation process because we believe this is vital to the success of the newly placed executive. We also provide clients and candidates with a helpful book called *New Role, New Reality* by Dr. John Burdett.

While successful integration is much more complex, the basic message is that the job of a candidate's successful integration into their new role and new company is the responsibility of both the candidate and the company that hired them. Indeed, we have found that a new hire has the greatest chance of success when both parties the candidate and the client take responsibility for the integration process.

When tracking candidate performance it is important to track the candidate's view and not just the hiring authority's perception. Countless surveys have been conducted along these lines. Here are the results of a recent study published in ExecuNet.

Executives Rate Attributes Most Responsible For Their Career Success

1. Ability to achieve objectives.............................….. 21.2%
2. The value of my professional work....................…..... 13.7%
3. Impact on company's financial performance.......….. 13.5%
4. Relationships with superiors...........…................….....12.0%
5. Ability to develop and retain key talent on my team...11.5%
6. Educational background..................…...................... 9.0%
7. Willingness to accept developmental assignments......7.9%
8. My willingness to relocate during my career.............. 6.2%
9. Advanced training I have received in my function...... 3.0%
10. Other....................…............................…...................1.4%

A clear understanding of how highly experienced business professionals view their career successes can give you powerful insight as they formulate search and recruiting, as well as retention strategies.

According to Dr. Burdett, recent research suggests that at least 40 percent of those moving in to a new role struggle. For CEO's the statistic is closer to 60 percent. John is a Canadian consultant with whom our consulting organization has a relationship. He has written some of the best material I have ever read on leadership, culture and executive integration. Not surprisingly, Canadian statistics are almost identical to those we have observed in America.

There are a number of reasons why executives derail when they move in to a new role. Inadequate definition of the role, poor recruitment practices and lack of openness during the hiring process all play their part. High on any list of why those moving into a new role stumble, however, is that they are given little or no support during the crucial integration period.

This omission is quite remarkable when you think about the overall cost of hiring, and/or the additional cost of having someone in a leadership role who is struggling to find his or her feet. The reality: the faster an executive integrates in to the new role, the faster he or she can begin to produce value for the organization. The challenge: the time that an executive is given to prove him/herself is getting ever shorter.

Integration support also has a significant impact on leadership retention. Talented people stay with an organization for all sorts of reasons: the reputation of the organization, a sense of accomplishment, freedom to act, the feeling that he/she is making a difference. More important than anything else, however, is the quality of learning offered by the organization. It is a perception that is created, for better or for worse, as soon as a new executive joins the organization.

For the established executive, that initial feeling is revisited every time he or she moves in to a new role. Lack of support during those early and anxious days mean not only a costly waiting period while the new executive gets up to speed, but it may well mean the loss of that executive the next time he or she is courted. At a time of dramatic shortfalls in leadership talent, these are business issues that cannot be ignored.

In talking about executive integration, we are not limited to those who move between organizations - although this is an important issue. Merger and acquisition means that many of the key roles change, and change dramatically. An organization going through what is often referred to as "culture change" of necessity redefines the role of every leader in the organization. A move to another country even where, at first glance, the work seems to be the same, invariably means that the role has changed. Promotion, internal transfer, and new leadership challenge mean that the leader in question has to think anew his or her role.

Need executive integration be problematical? Need there be a 40 percent failure rate? The answer is a resounding NO! Having said that, without a new approach, little will change. A better way is possible only if the organization introduces the tools that allow the new executive to take responsibility for his or her own integration. Equally important, a better way is possible only where the new executive is given a clear path to follow.

Those who successfully move in to a new role quickly realize that flexibility, openness and a willingness to learn are the name of the game. The new executive must become the observer of his/her own behavior, to ask new questions and to draw new insights from the experience.

Not so long ago the term executive would have applied only to a relatively small group of "top" people. Today, with the flattening of organizational structures, the pushing of decision-making closer to the customer, the term "executive" should rightfully be applied to anyone who has the opportunity to shape the nature and breadth of their contribution.

Executives, in the modern organization, thus do not necessarily carry glamorous titles nor operate out of a prestigious office along mahogany row. An executive is simply someone who, through initiative, creativity and a willingness to act, makes a significant difference to the way the company creates value for its customers. Using this definition means that executives can be found at every level and in all parts of the organization.

Executive integration is an important issue. It is also a practical issue. If you have just moved in to a new role, you cannot afford to fail. If you are the hiring executive, you cannot afford anything less than total success.

For the new executive, around every turn there is a large hole filled with muddy water and the new executive in his/her new shoes! A new course: Where did this wind come from? No one mentioned these frequent gusts. And everywhere else, silence! Where is that guy that coached you out the door?

Then there is the landing. Even those who have made many jumps can crash on landing. Executives faced with a new role will, if forced to be candid, confess to experiencing a range of emotions, most of them negative. Words like "confusing," "chaotic," "frustrating," and "overwhelming" come mixed with phrases like "there is no one to talk to," "you would not believe how they...."

Put simply, moving into or assuming a new role is a difficult period in any executive's working life, and he or she enters into the new situation feeling profoundly at risk. Get it right, successfully scramble through the early days, and the feelings of inadequacy quickly fade. Get it wrong and those early negative impressions concerning the organization and his or her place within it, will be very difficult to overcome. A few wrong turns during the integration period can take an executive off the corporate map and into hostile territory.

Getting the best out of the integration opportunity is really about **attitude.** It is about emotional commitment and being willing to see what others describe as a burden, as a rich learning experience. The real spirit, and thus mastery, of executive integration lays in the belief that confusion, frustration and occasional bouts of depression are merely the price to pay for **a unique opportunity to better know one's self.**

The good news is executive integration does not have to be a debilitating experience. It need not be a combination of scavenger hunt and obstacle course. Those who have framed each integration experience as a self-development opportunity, those who have found the techniques for coping and the strategies for achieving, have discovered that success in a new role is ultimately a process that, like any other, can be learned.

Without getting too poetic, a worthwhile integration process unfolds much like a flower when it receives sunlight. The flower cannot move into full bloom, however, unless the soil is rich enough to sustain its growth. The nurturing mix that sustains the integration process is emotional discipline and positive self-analysis characteristics that are critical to the first stage of integration: Letting Go and Setting a New Course.

This first stage of moving in to a new role is not an element of the process that once completed can be set aside. Those going through the integration process inevitably find themselves falling back into old ways of thinking and behaving. The executive will be tempted, simply because of his or her new workload, to put integration as a specific activity on the back burner. Doing so allows those old patterns to re-emerge. The reality: energizing the integration process is an ever-present challenge.

One might look to a number of people and places for support during a change in role. Clearly the search consultant - assuming there is one - should play a role, as should the Human Resource executive involved. The hiring executive has a strong vested interest. Colleagues, subordinates, and customers also have a stake in the new executive's success. Yet, there is really only one place where responsibility rests, only one person to whom failure can be a lasting setback and only one person who can truly make it happen: the executive who, as a result of transfer, promotion, acquisition, merger, selection, or simply as a consequence of ongoing change, finds that he/she is faced with the reality of success in a new role.

Others *can and should* provide support. A mentor can be the source of new questions and insights. The hiring executive can help identify potholes in the road ahead. But only the new executive is in the position to put it all together.

Our orientation, our current ways of behaving, our mind-sets (mental models) regarding a new role, are the outcome of a series of competing emotional forces:

- What worked in the past
- The executive's view of an ideal future
- Early signals about what success looks like
- The executive's values and beliefs
- Role models from previous business experience

During the integration process, the new executive is operating at a heightened level of awareness. This extreme sense of the new reality is both necessary and, paradoxically, potentially damaging; necessary because the new executive is after all crossing new terrain and potentially damaging because as a direct result of this heightened sense, insecurity starts to creep in and with it the propensity to default in favor of past behavior. What is often misunderstood is the extent to which what worked in the past can be, and often is, a barrier to developing new ways to act and think.

The implications for those moving in to a new role are profound. Previous experience and past assumption of success become the filters through which new opportunities are judged. Established ways to be, and past solutions become, the "established tools of the trade" and are presumed to have primacy regardless of the situation.

By way of example it is not at all unusual for executives, even a year or more into a new role, to continue to refer to past experience as the basis for proposed change in the new organization: "Let me tell you how we did this in my past organization." In doing so, the individual concerned is not only unknowingly alienating his/her new colleagues, but through frames of reference telling others, "I'm not sure if I want to be part of this team." The message they give out is that their head and their hand may be committed to the new role but their heart and spirit lays elsewhere.

The new executive must be willing to let go of language, especially metaphors that present imagery that is misaligned with the new culture. Metaphors that strike male images ("we have to put the puck in the net this time") in an environment where a high percentage of the team are women; win-lose language ("kill the competition") where the business environment is one highly dependent upon alliances; and language that frames performance as being the prerogative of individual success but where the climate is one highly dependent upon the team ("when the ice is thin success goes to the fastest skater") all serve to set the new executive apart, all significantly limit what is possible. For a leader language is not merely important - language is everything! Language gives potency to an idea, language energizes, language engages, language provides meaning, and language translates concepts into action. But only if it is the *right language!*

Integration, when everything else is stripped away, is about two things: the ability to fit in and the ability to manage expectations. Inappropriate behavior with regard to either can lead to difficulties. Managing expectations ultimately comes down to the nature, quality and timing of delivery. Fit is another matter altogether.

Fit has largely to do with overall presentation, personal style, orientation, language and pace. The higher the quality of the gem, the more time and effort needs to be spent on crafting the setting. Fit begins as an issue before the start date for the new role. Fit is a feature of the integration equation from the very first time there is contact. It is a product of trust, sensitivity and, above all else, awareness. From the very first interaction the new executive needs to have his/her antennae fully extended. An outstanding salesman or saleswoman does this naturally. Indeed, top sales people are the grand masters of political astuteness. Similarly, the new executive needs to become quickly attuned to his or her new political and social environment.

Past experience can be both a source of strength, and the source of what often amounts to a skewed view of the new reality. Some specialists, for example, are invariably skilled at identifying the fiscal or technical issues but lack judgment when it comes to people. And make no mistake, fit is a "people issue".

There are many things that the new executive should be assessing. The following questions, however, loom high in any assessment of fit. How does this organization create value for its customers, does moving in to the new role entail for me new ways to think, to act, and to feel? How is the company organized, is there a well-defined strategy, what is it, what stories are being told, what systems dominate? What values are implied by the behavior I come across, what gets measured, how do teams act, what is the commitment to teamwork, how do teams communicate with other teams? How do key individuals behave, what seems to drive them, what do they talk about, where, and on what, is there a real focus (discipline)?

Fit is a two-way process. Starting to understand what drives the organization and how people behave is not the same as fit. The new executive needs not only to be conscious of how others behave, but to be acutely aware of his or her own actions. He or she needs to put him or herself into the shoes of those he or she meets, and ask "how does this person perceive me?", "what sort of individual does he or she think I am?"

Learning to let go and settling is the ability to move into someone else's body and see the world from their point of view. Also key is the ability to step back from the ongoing communication and become both participant and observer. In third position, the individual displays an ability to interpret the ongoing interpersonal dance, and anticipate moves in order to lead or follow as desired.

Fit is the positive outcome of heightened awareness. Fit is about listening. It is, ultimately, about making personal adjustment - something that is highly unlikely if the new executive is stuck in first position. Gathering information is a first position attribute. Awareness, knowing **and** acting with purpose are possible only if the new executive moves comfortably and elegantly, as needed, through all three positions.

A move into a new role is a little like traveling to a new country. At the point of departure, everything is compatible. The language is easy to understand and if something goes wrong, knowing how to get it fixed is relatively straightforward. Upon arrival, everything changes. There is a new language to contend with. There are new customs and new ways to get things done. Even the police cannot be assumed to have the same priorities. The likelihood is that even the climate will be different. If the plane is delayed and plans have been disrupted, panic is not an uncommon response.

Arrival is a far less stressful experience if a friend or colleague who knows the environment is waiting on the tarmac. With an intra-company move, that is indeed a possibility. For an executive moving into a new organization, it is far less likely.

For a politician to get elected and hold power, he or she must have a constituency of support. For executives to even start to compete at the highest level, they too must be given support. Without a network even the brightest and best executives are destined to get lost. Without a constituency the new executive will feel as if they have wandered into a constantly reconfiguring maze.

A constituency, of course, is exactly what the new executive **does not** have. He or she, therefore, needs to build one - an untenable goal if the new executive sits in his or her office waiting for the world to knock on the door.

John Burdett says much more about executive integration in our favorite book and roadmap for our role in executive integration, or on-boarding *New Role New Reality*.

EIGHTEEN

Ending the CEO Succession Crisis (HBR)

We talk about leadership as though leaders, like Tolstoy's happy families are all alike. But CEO leadership should be a subject apart because it is unique in scope and substance and of incomparable importance. CEOs' performance determines the fates of corporations, which collectively influence whole economies. Our standard of living depends upon excellence at the very top.

Who, then, would dispute that CEO selection deserves perpetual front-burner attention from the custodians of a company's welfare? Surely, when time or trauma ushers in change, organizations should be ready with a clear view of current and future needs and with carefully tended pools of candidates.

But they are not. The CEO succession process is broken in North America and is no better in many other parts of the world. Almost half of companies with revenue greater than $500 million have no meaningful CEO succession plan, according to the National Association of Corporate Directors. Even those that have plans are not happy with them. The Corporate Leadership Council (CLC), a human resource research organization, surveyed 276 large companies last year and found that only 20 percent of responding HR executives were satisfied with their top-management succession processes.

That deficiency is simply inexcusable. A CEO or board that has been in place for six or seven years and has not yet provided a pool of qualified candidates, and a robust process for selecting the next leader, is a failure. Everyone talks about emulating such best practitioners as General Electric, but few work very hard at it

The result of poor succession planning is often poor performance, which translates into higher turnover and corporate instability. CEO tenures continue to shrink as increased transparency, more vocal institutional investors, and more active boards make greater demands. Booz Allen Hamilton reports that the global average CEO tenure is now just 7.6 years, down from 9.5 years in 1995. Two out of every five new CEOs fail in the first 18 months, as Dan Ciampa cites in his article "Almost Ready" in last month's HBR.

The problem is not just that more CEOs are being replaced. The problem is that, in many cases, CEOs are being replaced badly. Too often, new leaders are plucked from the well-worn Rolodexes of a small recruiting oligarchy and appointed by directors who have little experience hiring anyone for a position higher than COO, vice chairman, CFO, or president of a large business unit. Hiring a CEO is simply different.

Coaxing former leaders out of retirement is another popular way to fill the void. Celebrated examples include Harry Stonecipher at Boeing, Bill Stavropoulos of Dow Chemical, and Jamie Houghton at Corning. But most "boomerang CEOs" returns for just a couple of years, long enough to restore credibility and put a real succession candidate in place. They are not the long-term solution.

To increase their chances of finding a leader who will serve long and well, companies must do three things. First, they should have available a deep pool of internal candidates kept well stocked by a leadership development process that reaches from the bottom to the top. Second, boards should create, then continually update and refine a succession plan and have in place a thoughtful process for making decisions about candidates. Finally, directors considering outside candidates should be exacting, informed drivers of the executive search process, leading recruiters rather than being led by them.

In my 35 years advising corporations, I have participated in dozens of CEO selections and have closely monitored numerous executive pipelines. Drawing on that experience, I will in these pages first explain why companies make poor appointments, and then suggest what they can instead do to make good ones. Using these guidelines, organizations can ensure that all participants, directors, executive recruiters, and sitting CEOs perform wisely and appropriately when it comes time to choose their next leader.

The Trouble with Outsiders

When companies lack the culture or the processes to grow their own heirs apparent, they have no choice but to look outside. More than a third (37 percent) of the Fortune 1,000 companies are run by external recruits, according to the public affairs firm Burson-Marsteller. Although global data are harder to come by, the worldwide trend appears to be similar. But external candidates are in most cases a greater risk because directors and top management cannot know them as well as they know their own people.

Outsiders are generally chosen because they can do a job turn around the company or restructure the portfolio. But the job is to lead a hugely complex organization over many years through an unpredictable progression of shifting markets and competitive terrains. Unfortunately, the requirements for that larger job are often not well defined by the board, which may be focused on finding a savior.

The results are not surprising. In North America, 55 percent of outside CEOs who departed in 2003 were forced to resign by their boards, compared with 34 percent of insiders, Booz Allen reports. In Europe, 70 percent of departing outsiders got the boot, compared with 55 percent of insiders. Some outside CEOs are barely around long enough to see their photographs hung in the headquarters lobby. Gil Amelio left Apple 17 months after he arrived from National Semiconductor. Ex-IBMer Richard Thoman was out of the top spot at Xerox after 13 months. David Siegel gave up the wheel at Avis Rent A Car for US Airways but departed two years later.

Even under the best circumstances, CEO selection is something of a batting average: Companies will not hit successfully every time.

But two or more consecutive outsider outs can have a devastating effect on employees, partners, and strategic position. New leaders import new teams and management styles. Continuity and momentum collapse, the energy to execute dwindles, and morale plummets as employees obsess about who will get the next pink slip. Rather than focus on the competition, companies starts to look inward. Bad external appointments are also expensive, since even poor performance is rewarded with rich severance packages.

The Trouble with Insiders

On the other hand, sometimes an external candidate exists who is, very simply, the best available choice. A skillful, diligent board may discover an outstanding fit between an outsider and the job at hand. Lou Gerstner and IBM spring to mind. Boards must remember that just as outsiders are not uniformly bad choices, insiders are not uniformly good ones. In certain situations, internal candidates actually present the greater risk.

Some concerns about insiders, ironically, emerge from their very closeness to the company. For example, as known quantities, they may sail through lax due diligence process. Or their social networks and psychological ties may complicate the culture. Some will not have had the right experience or been tested in the right ways. Individuals from functional areas may not be up to the task of leading the entire business. Or a shift in the industry or market landscape may render carefully nurtured skills irrelevant. In some cases, the credibility of the outgoing CEO or management team may be so sullied that only a new broom can sweep the company clean.

What is more, companies that have no ongoing senior management development program (currently more the rule than the exception) will in all probability need to look outside, maybe for as long as the next ten to twenty years. Outside candidates, in other words, should always be an option. But so long as they remain the only option, and the boards lack rigor in identifying and assessing them, succession is imperiled.

The Trouble with CEO Development

Many organizations do a decent job nurturing middle managers, but meaningful leadership development stops well below the apex. The problem manifests itself as a dearth of senior managers, for which companies must increasingly shop in other neighborhoods. Almost half of respondents to the CLC survey had hired a third or more of their senior executive teams from outside, but only 22 percent of those did so because they considered external candidates irresistibly appealing. Rather, 45 percent of all respondents judged that it would take too long or be too expensive to develop successors internally.

It is easy to understand why they feel that way. Even where strong development programs exist, very few leaders will ever be qualified to run the company, very few. A $25 billion corporation with 70,000 employees, for instance, may have 3,000 leaders, perhaps 50 to 100 of whom would qualify for one for one of the ten jobs just below the top. That same company would be fortunate to field five strong internal candidates for CEO – and two or three is a more realistic number. General Electric had around 225,000 workers in 1993 when Jack Welch identified 20 potential successors; over seven years, he winnowed the number to three. In CEO succession, it takes a ton of ore to produce an ounce of gold.

Furthermore, the window in which to spot CEO talent is narrow. Companies require sufficiently seasoned candidates who can be counted on to hold the top job for ten years or more. That puts the age of accession at between 46 and 52. In my experience, for a candidate to be ready by 46, serious development should start by age 30. Recognizing which five saplings in a 3,000-tree forest are the ones to nurture requires a degree of discernment that most line managers and HR departments lack and few are developing.

Some companies do identify candidates early but then fail to evaluate them properly. Such organizations often turn evaluation over to HR, which may rely excessively on packaged databases of leadership traits developed by researchers in the human behavior field. Those programs compare internal high potentials with generic benchmarks along many dimensions, a process that creates fragmented profiles of some cookie-cutter ideal rather than nuanced, individualized portraits. What is more, most of those dimensions reflect only the personality traits and not the skills required of a CEO.

Nor do many companies properly nurture the candidates they identify. Some misjudge the business's needs and consequently emphasize the wrong talents. Only 24 percent of organizations the CLC surveyed believe their leadership development efforts are aligned with their strategic goals. And those goals can be a moving target, changing in response to sometimes tectonic shifts in the external environment, the marketplace change, and technology changes. Employees' skills become obsolete even as they develop. What is more, very few in-house executive education programs are designed to impart the skills and know-how that a CEO needs.

But the larger issue is that true development happens on the job, not in a classroom. Few companies know how to get their best people the experiences that would prepare them for the CEO role or to rigorously evaluate them in the jobs they do perform. Many companies, for example, still equate leadership development with circulating candidates through multiple functions. In the 1970s, that was the rule at AT&T, IBM, and Xerox, companies that produced- leaders who went on to become CEOs elsewhere and in some cases failed.

The problem with that approach is that potential candidates do not stay long enough in one position to live with the consequences of their decisions. In addition, functional leaders learn to lead functions, not whole companies. Faced with external competition, they fall back on their functional expertise. You can mine all possible lessons from a turn as Vice President of Marketing and still be blindsided by a Profit & Loss Report.

The Trouble with Boards

Bob Stemple's short stint as the head of General Motors ended ingloriously in 1992 and so did the accepted wisdom that boards should automatically bless the departing CEO's hand-picked successor.

Yet while directors describe CEO succession as one of their most consuming issues, they do not appear consumed by it. In a survey by Mercer Delta and the University of Southern California, 40 percent of corporate directors called their involvement in CEO succession planning less than optimal. (I would hazard to add that far fewer are satisfied with the outcome of their involvement.) Only 21 percent responded that they were satisfied with their level of participation in developing internal candidates for senior management

A packed agenda is the chief culprit Governance and fiduciary duties, in particular, command an outsize share of boards' attention. Mercer Delta asked directors to compare the amount of time they spend now with the amount they spent a year earlier on nine key activities. Large majorities reported devoting more or many more hours to monitoring accounting, Sarbanes-Oxley, risk, and financial performance. They also reported spending less time interacting with and preparing potential CEO successors than on any other activity. Yet boards' work on succession represents probably 80 percent of the value they deliver. If the choice of CEO successor is superb, all subsequent decisions become easier.

Another huge problem is that the vast majority of search committee members have had no experience working together on a CEO succession. As a result, they seldom coalesce into deep-delving bodies that get to the pith of their companies' fundamental needs. So they end up approaching their search with only the demands of the moment or worse the broadest of requirements.

As they audition candidates, directors may be seduced by reputation, particularly if they are considering a Wall Street or media darling. A few aspiring CEOs employ publicists who flog rosy stories to journalists; when those leaders are up for other jobs, their press bestowed halos follow them. Board members can also be blinded by charisma, by the sheer star quality of a candidate. There is nothing intrinsically wrong with charisma, though some criticize it as the sheep's clothing in which hubris lurks. But too often directors become so focused on what candidates are like that they do not press hard enough to discover what candidates can and cannot do.

For example, one board looking for a new CEO after firing the old one asked for someone who could build a great team and get things done. The recruiter presented such a person an energetic, focused candidate whose personal qualities quickly won over directors. What the organization really needed was someone who could create a stream of new products and win shelf space from powerful retailers in a volatile marketplace. Unfortunately, the directors never specified those requirements, or raised them either during interviews or the background check.

The candidate's upstream-marketing skills were poor to nonexistent. The company's market share declined precipitously, and three years later the CEO was out on his ear. On its second try, the board concentrated so hard on marketing that it ignored execution. The next CEO was a visionary and a marketing genius but was unable to get things done. The company, once first in its market, will probably be sold or stumble into Chapter 11.

Finally, directors too often shunt due diligence to recruiters. As a result, that process can be quite superficial. One company that left vetting to its recruiter and investment banker found itself saddled with a leader who botched critical people issues. At a postmortem three years later, directors discovered that at his former company the CEO had routinely punted people problems to the chairman, who had been CEO before him and occupied the office next to his. That would have been nice to know before the pen touched the contract.

The Trouble with Recruiters

Executive recruiters are honest and highly professional. Still, they can wield disproportionate influence in CEO succession decisions. One reason is concentration. Just three recruiters control some 80 percent of the Fortune 100 CEO search market (a single firm claims fully 60 percent of it), and one or two people within those companies direct the most important searches. These firms' social networks are vast and powerful. Anyone with a smidgen of ambition in the corporate world knows whom they have to know to get ahead.

At the same time, board members' inexperience and consequent inability to precisely define their needs makes recruiters' task difficult. Recruiters must satisfy their clients yet also manage them, helping the search committee to gel so they can extract the criteria they need while keeping requirements broad enough to cast the widest talent net possible.

When committees do not gel, recruiters may step into the vacuum with their own criteria, and directors too often let them. Unfortunately, no executive recruiter can grasp the subtleties of a client's business as well as the client can. In the absence of effective direction, recruiters generally approach each search with a boilerplate of the 20 or so attributes they consider most desirable for any CEO. That formula tends to overemphasize generic qualities like character and vision, as well as team-building, change-management, and relationship skills. Psychology and chemistry are also very important to executive recruiters: Like directors, they may let a personality surplus overshadow a skills deficit

In one granted, extreme case, the longtime CEO of a company with four highly successful businesses and a huge debt level was retiring. The recruiter produced a list of six candidates, pressing one the head of a very large division at a multinational company-hard on the board. Yet all the recruiter gave the directors was a page-and-a-half description of this candidate's leadership skills; a list of his extensive connections with unions, customers, and government bodies; and an outline of his swift rise through the organization.

A financial performance history for the candidate's division was not included and not publicly available, so a member of the search committee began to dig. He discovered that return on assets under the candidate's supervision was minuscule over the previous five years, even though his division was four times larger than the entire company considering him for CEO. Furthermore, this man had never earned cost of capital in his life. Even so, the recruiter wanted to put him in charge of a business that had certainly done so and that hoped to rise to the next level.

Fortunately, after much debate, the committee vetoed the recommendation, opting instead for number three on the recruiter's list the president of another company, who had consistently improved performance and delivered a 20 percent return on equity, his first three years, this new CEO took the stock from 24 to 108 in a slow-moving industry. The board was happy. Management was happy. The recruiter's preferred candidate was happy when he was placed at another, larger company but then he was fired in six months.

Executive recruiters also succumb to the usual-suspects bias, primarily looking for new heads above other companies' necks. It is just plain easier to compile a list of sitting CEOs than to make a case for or take a risk on a COO or an executive VP. Some recruiters go so far as to approach sitting CEOs, even with no specific jobs to dangle, and urge them to consider looking elsewhere. The recruiters' goal is to loosen a prized gem from its setting and thereby beat a fellow recruiter to the punch.

Sometimes, the board's selection of recruiter is flawed from the start a director may jump the gun, recommending a recruiter he has worked well with even before the search committee is formed. Nor do most boards examine search firms' track records, that is, how many of the CEOs the firm has placed have succeeded and how many have failed. Even if directors did ask that question, they are not likely to get the answer because it appears no one is monitoring recruiters' performance. The stock-buying public, by contrast, knows exactly how well directors score on their CEO choices.

How to Succeed at Succession

Charlie Bell's ascension to the top spot at McDonald's within hours of Jim Cantalupo's death reflected well on a company that had its house in order, particularly when compared as it inevitably was with Coca-Cola's simultaneous travails. Similarly, NBC's early, orderly announcement that Brian Williams would replace network news anchor Tom Brokaw stands in stark relief to CBS's public uncertainty over Dan Rather's successor. (Anchors are not CEOs, of course, but they are even more visible and arguably as consequential to their organizations' fortunes.)

By now it should be clear that the most important thing companies can do to improve succession is to bolster their leadership development and focus on those very rare people in their ranks who might one day be CEO. Organizations must identify high-potential candidates early in their careers, and global companies must look in all the countries where they operate. As candidates enter the development pipeline, managers must constantly align their charges' education and on-the-job experience with the emerging landscape; they must rigorously assess the candidates' performance at each developmental stage.

The very best preparation for CEOs is progression through positions with responsibility for steadily larger and more complex Profit & Loss centers. A candidate might start by managing a single product, then a customer segment, then a country, then several product lines, then a business unit, and then a division. Whatever the progression, Profit & Loss responsibility at every level is key. The Thomson Corporation, a global provider of information solutions, comprises more than 100 P&L's, so its top people have abundant opportunity to run a $50 million to $100 million business. "That is the best crucible for formulating leaders that I know of," says Jim Smith, executive vice president of human resources and administration.

Companies not set up to provide such opportunities should create jobs large projects or small internal organizations that exercise the Profit & Loss muscle. Otherwise, they risk elevating an internal candidate who is not prepared. For example, one $10 billion company in a highly capital-intensive and unionized industry has targeted as CEO successor the head of its smallest division. The candidate is a brilliant, articulate young man but has no experience running a big business in general or this type of business in particular (his own division is knowledge intensive, and unionized labor has no presence). The board is considering creating a deputy position within its largest division for this person and making the 59-year-old current division head (who will retire in three years) his coach, granting that coach a bonus if he ensures his successor's success.

Companies with inflexible functional structures will probably be forced to import Profit & Loss - tested leaders from outside and place them in very high positions. To reduce the risk, they should bring in such executives three or four years before the expected succession. That can be challenging, however, because many will demand appointment to the top spot in less than a year.

But leadership development is just part of the solution. Boards, too, can greatly improve the chances of finding a strong successor by acting vigilantly before and during the search. Senior executive development should be overseen by the board's compensation and organization committee, which needs to receive periodic reports on the entire pool of potential CEOs and regular updates on those bobbing near the top of it The committee should spend a third of its time examining lists of the top 20 candidates in the leadership pipeline. In addition, at least 15 percent of the 60 or so hours that members meet as a full board should be devoted to succession. At minimum, the board ought to dedicate two sessions a year to hashing over at least five CEO candidates, both internal and external.

And directors should personally get to know the company's rising stars. Promising leaders should be invited to board meetings, to the dinners that precede board meetings, and members should talk with them informally whenever possible. Directors should also meet with and observe candidates within the natural habitats of their business operations. In this way, when it comes time to single out CEO candidates, directors will be considering a set of very well-known quantities.

The "Fit" Imperative

The goal of all these interactions and deliberations is for board members to reach a highly refined but dynamic understanding of the CEO position and their options for it long before appointing a successor. Company leaders should be as well defined as puzzle pieces; their strengths and experiences must match the shape of their organizations' needs. That is, they simply must fit. Boards achieve fit by specifying, in terms as precise as possible, three or four aspects of talent, know-how, and experience that are non-negotiable.

Ideally, these attributes pertain to the organization's dominant needs for the next several years, but they should also relate to future growth. In one recent CEO succession, the company, in conjunction with a boutique recruiting firm, began with impossibly broad criteria that included everything from industry leader to change agent The process floundered until the search committee narrowed its focus to three qualities: experience in segmenting markets according to customer needs, the talent to grow the business organically and a track record of building strong executive teams. Those three skills, in addition to general leadership traits, delineated the pond in which this company fished.

The job of defining such qualities belongs to the search committee, which should form well before succession is scheduled to take place. As they wrestle with requirements, committee members must constantly keep in mind the company's changing circumstances, so that an understanding of what currently works does not congeal into what works, period.

For example, Bank of America flourished for years under deal maker par excellence Hugh McColl, Jr. But by the time he stepped down in 2001, integration, rather than acquisition, had become the dominant challenge. Having recognized the altered environment several years before, BOA's board chose not a leader in McColl's image but instead Ken Lewis, a company veteran proficient at integration of acquisitions and organic growth. (For an example of how a company integrates its leadership development with its strategy, see the sidebar "The Living Succession Tree.")

Specific, nonnegotiable criteria also let directors keep control when they work with executive recruiters. With good direction, search firms can be a valuable source of objectivity, benchmarking internal candidates against outsiders and making sure that board members consider all possibilities, even if they prefer an insider. Some companies even bring in recruiters to do independent assessments of insider candidates. Their concurrence with a board's judgment carries weight with shareholders and potential critics.

Search firms ask boards to recommend candidates, and they take those recommendations seriously. But, ultimately, it is the recruiter who compiles the list, and the compiler of the list wields considerable influence. Directors must require from recruiters detailed explanations of how the candidates fulfill their criteria. A ten-page report on each is reasonable.

When the time comes to select the new CEO, directors ordinarily a polite breed, unaccustomed to challenging one another or asking discomforting questions must engage in a vigorous discussion of the candidates' comparative merits. One search committee that did an outstanding job making the final decision invited five candidates (two internal and three external) to a hotel for a couple of days. The two internal candidates were favorites of two different directors. On the first day, the committee interviewed three candidates, two external, and one internal. The directors split into two groups of three, and each group spoke with one candidate for 90 minutes. After these interviews, the directors broke for 45 minutes to share impressions, then switched candidates. Then the two groups of directors took turns interviewing the third candidate, similarly sharing impressions informally. At the end of the first day, the committee members debated over dinner, and the director who had originally advocated for the internal candidate *volunteered that he was indeed not the strongest choice. The next day, they repeated the process with the two other candidates, and the results were remarkably the same, with the director who had originally advocated for the internal candidate changing his mind. In the course of these discussions, all hidden agendas fell away, requirements were honed, and directors were able to reach consensus.*

Finally, board members must do due diligence on outside candidates and do it well. Directors must seek reliable external sources and demand candor from them. Board members should ask first about the candidate's natural talents. If those gifts admirable as they may be do not match the position's specific profile, that candidate is not worth pursuing. Needless to say, due diligence is also the time to root out any fatal character flaws.

At this point, the role of the outgoing CEO is chiefly consultative. He or she must be active in spotting and grooming talent, help define the job's requirements, provide accurate information about both internal and external candidates, and facilitate discussions between candidates and directors. But when the choice of successor is imminent, make no mistake: that decision belongs to the board.

Inside a Development Engine

Despite the current crisis, we know it is possible to build organizations that reliably produce great CEO's. Starting after World War II, a few corporations emerged as veritable leadership factories. Companies like General Electric, Emerson Electric, Sherwin-Williams, Procter & Gamble, and Johnson & Johnson managed to stock not only their own corner offices but also many others. (Of course even great companies sometimes stumble: Procter & Gamble had a failure from within when it promoted Durk Jager to the top spot, but it is going great guns under the stewardship of company veteran A.G. Lafley.)

Reuben Mark has sat atop Colgate-Palmolive for 20 years, so the company's CEO succession chops have not been recently proven.

But I believe the consumer products giant has a first-rate process for identifying and developing CEO talent at the very least it produced three internal candidates who are excellent prospects for the job.

Colgate-Palmolive does business in more than 200 countries; its emerging leaders are correspondingly international and diverse. Leadership evaluation begins during the first year of employment. "It may seem strange to talk about someone who has been here just a year when discussing the pipeline to the CEO," says Bob Joy, senior vice president of global human resources. "But the earlier you start to identify talent, the earlier you can provide the job assignments and develop the broad business experience needed by a CEO candidate."

Each subsidiary identifies its own high potentials and submits that list to local general managers, who add and subtract names and then hand the list off to the division heads. These lists wind their way up the chain until they reach the Colgate-Palmolive Human Resource (CPHR) committee, composed of Colgate's CEO, president, COO, the senior VP of HR, and the senior candidates up for the top job. CPHR modifies and consolidates the lists into a single master list, dispatching it back down the ranks where managers can contest decisions made by those above them The process takes place once a year.

Those who make the cut are deployed in one of three tracks. The first track, local talent, is for relatively junior staff who might become the direct reports of a general manager. Someone more advanced would be designated regional talent, and given, for example, a significant position in Asia. The most elevated track global talent is the reservoir from which the most senior jobs are filled. Throughout their careers, all these high potentials receive assignments that stretch their abilities and expand their knowledge, exposing them to a variety of markets, cultures, consumers, and business circumstances. CPHR itself designs career paths for general managers and higher positions because the committee is at the same time dynamically developing the profile of Colgate's future leadership team. (Also, says Joy, "you can *imagine the kind of resistance you'd get from a division president who would like to keep his high-potential people in his own area.") The thousand or so highest high potentials (out of a total pool of about 2,000) receive outside executive coaching, which includes 360-degree feedback on current and past assignments.*

Having identified its high potentials, Colgate strives to bolster its connection to the company. One tactic is recognition: "If you are talking about the future leaders of your company, you want them to feel special," says Joy. "You want them to have Colgate in their veins." Toward that end, the company sponsors a series of "visibility programs." One, for example, gathers high potentials from all over the world at Colgate's New York headquarters for week-long sessions during which they meet with every senior leader in the company. In addition, each high potential receives a special stock grant, which arrives with a personal letter from the CEO.

Colgate's global growth program mandates that all senior managers retain 90 percent of their high potentials or lose some compensation. If a high potential at any level, anywhere in the world, does resign, the CEO, the COO, the president, and Joy are alerted within 24 hours and move immediately to retain that person.

Perhaps most important, Joy collaborates with the office of the chairman to connect directors early and often with high potentials in all areas. At the most senior level, functional leaders introduce the board to the top two or three most-promising heirs for their own positions, adding detailed analyses of those candidates' strengths and weaknesses. Emerging leaders routinely take part in presentations to the board and meet informally with directors over lunch. Board members closely track the progress not of one or two people but of the top 200, frequently discussing how each piece fits into the puzzle and what experiences or skills might improve that fit.

As a result, when CEO succession looms, the board and top management will be able to select from candidates they have spent many, many years observing and evaluating. "If you start five years or even ten years before the CEO is going to retire," says Joy, "it may be too late."

Of course Colgate-Palmolive like General Electric tackles succession from a position of strength. Its CEO has been two decades in the saddle, and he is passionate on the subject of an heir. Companies with less-veteran chiefs and whose boards have been negligent in this area will probably need to line up candidates quickly, while laying a deeper pipeline. They will in all likelihood have to bring in outsiders and position them to gain the requisite business and industry experience. That may mean shaking up the leadership team and reporting structures to free up slots in which outsiders can be tested. This restructuring will probably be resented, but it is necessary pain.

A quick infusion of talent may be a company's only course, but it is no way to run a railroad. Organizations without meaningful pipelines must start now to put them in place. Young companies should create the processes that will come to fruition in five or ten years' time. Choosing the CEO's successor is not one decision but the amalgam of thousands of decisions made by many people every day over years and years. Such meticulous, steady attention to defining needs and evaluating candidates produces strong leaders and inspires succession planners at lower levels to exercise the same discipline.

The trend of CEO failures must be reversed. CEO succession is all boards' paramount responsibility, nothing else so profoundly affects their companies' futures. Directors must start investing their time and energy today. The call for a new leader could come tomorrow.

The Living Succession Tree

Four years ago, top management at the Thomson Corporation realized that its CEO succession process had passed out of life and into a stagnant existence on paper. Leadership development chugged along separately from business planning. Human resource groups produced reams of documents and charts dense with the branches of succession trees. "We never used them," says Jim Smith, executive vice president of human resources and administration at the $7 billion global company." I never saw anybody go to a chart and say, 'Let us look at this.'"

So the company decided to rethink talent management in order to field leaders who could run Thomson under whatever conditions might exist. The new process is built on two principles: Succession planning should happen in lockstep with strategy making, and the current CEO should be intimately and visibly involved.

Each February, Thomson's 200 top managers gather to review corporate initiatives. Then in April, CEO Richard Harrington, CFO Robert Daleo, and Smith conduct strategy reviews with emerging leaders in every business unit. Goals coming out of those talks related to markets, customers, products, and growth areas accompany the trio into the next round of discussions, which takes place in June and focuses on management development.

At that point, Harrington, Daleo, and Smith devote eight full days to listening to senior executives (including CEO candidates) report on their highest potentials. The trio insists on concrete examples throughout. "It is so easy to generalize on how somebody's doing: 'He's a good guy' and 'She's terrific with people'" says Smith."We want to pin down the facts beneath that. 'You say she's good with people. Give me some examples of who she's developed. How many have been promoted?'"

The same people who attended the strategy meetings attend the leadership development meetings, so everyone in the room understands what talent the business requires. And when those same people reconvene again a few months later to discuss budgets, conclusions from the strategy and leadership development rounds inform their decisions. By year's end, Thomson has tightly integrated strategy, leadership, and budget plans. And Harrington and his senior team have spent many, many hours getting to know the company's most-promising CEO candidates.

Smith has three recommendations for companies interested in crafting a similar system, which has proved constructive to managers and the board alike. First, make sure the CEO devotes considerable personal time to identifying, getting to know, and developing leaders. Second, treat leadership development as part of the process used to run the business. Finally, make the process informal enough to encourage conversation. "We used to produce books," says Smith. "Now we have conversations."

This article by Ram Charan was published in the February 2005 edition of Harvard Business Review. While I promised not to include a litany of outside research and studies, Ram's article says basically the same thing we have been saying for many years from a slightly different perspective.

I sincerely hope the material contained in these pages is helpful to you and to your organization. Whether you are a hiring manager, search professional or candidate, I encourage you to think seriously about your processes for managing executive searches and your own career. If we may be of any further assistance, please feel free to contact any of our Partners through our website at www.allenaustinsearch.com or contact me directly at (713) 355-1900 extension 101.

Warmest Regards,

AUTHOR CONTACT INFORMATION:

Rob Andrews
Chairman & Chief Executive Officer

Allen Austin Global Executive Search
4543 Post Oak Place Drive, Suite 217
Houston, Texas 77027
randrews@allenaustinsearch.com
(713) 355-1900 ext. 101 Office
(713) 301-6130 Cell

AUTHOR BIOGRAPHY

Rob Andrews is Founder and Chief Executive Officer of Allen Austin Global Executive Search based in Houston, Texas. Rob is a widely respected consultant focused on what can best be described as "reinventing the search process." Rob has been building real world leadership teams since 1975 and has been a student and an innovator in the area of human capital leadership.

Rob is a human capital leadership aficionado and lends his passion for facilitating and building high performance teams to clients, consultants and candidates worldwide. He is always pushing the edge of the envelope to improve processes that produce high performance leadership teams and stellar business results.

Rob's personal consulting practice focuses on general management searches for a broad range of industries. His clients have run the gamut from $6 million privately held enterprises to $75+ billion publicly held multinational corporations. Rob has successfully completed searches at the CEO, COO, CFO and CTO level, as well as officer level searches in the functional areas of operations, marketing, merchandising, advertising, construction, facilities management, finance, accounting, systems, transportation, logistics, distribution, and security. Rob has personally conducted over 220 searches during his consulting career.

Prior to reentering the world of search in 1994, Rob served as regional vice president for Kash n' Karry Food Stores in Tampa,

Florida where he had total P&L responsibility for a region consisting of forty-nine supermarkets, three super-warehouse stores and thirty-one liquor stores. Rob also had responsibility for culture change management, service operations, training and for leading a major initiative to choreograph the customer's shopping experience.

Prior to his tenure at Kash n' Karry, Rob spent seven years with National Convenience Stores, rising from the level of area supervisor to division head in three years. During Rob's tenure at NCS, he had total responsibility for as many as 516 stores spread from El Paso, Texas to West Palm Beach, Florida. Rob consistently managed the top performing divisions in the company.

The early years in Rob's career included two years in search with Roth Young and thirteen years in retail, nine of which were spent with Safeway Stores Incorporated. In 1975, Rob became one of the youngest store managers in the history of the company. He quickly developed a reputation for his ability to drive sales and net profit in each of his six assignments as store manager.

Rob completed an undergraduate degree, attending classes on weekends, at Our Lady of the Lake University in San Antonio, Texas, while managing the southwestern division for National Convenience Stores in 1991. He subsequently completed his graduate work in business at the University of Texas at Austin in 1996 while serving as Executive Vice President of an east coast executive search firm. Rob completed the *Leading Professional Service Firms Program* at the Harvard Business School in 2007.

Allen Austin Global Executive Search was founded by Rob Andrews in 1996. The firm is unique among all search firms with its passion for facilitating matches that work and last. Allen Austin has followed through on over 2,000 retained engagements having never abandoned a single uncompleted assignment. Allen Austin has a 92 percent retention at the two year mark and a 97 percent offer/acceptance ratio. This is a result of the firm's rigorous process that has evolved over a period of thirty years of intensive study of hundreds of executive placements, successes and failures.

The Allen Austin FORESIGHT™ process endeavors to explore ALL critical success factors vital to long term success.

Allen Austin Global Executive Search is a member in good standing with The Association of Executive Search Firms (AESC). *Allen Austin is listed among the largest retained executive search consulting firms in Houston by the Houston Business Journal and has been ranked the #1 Executive Retained Search Firm in 2004, 2006, 2007 & 2008.*